Following Jesus in Invaded Space

Princeton Theological Monograph Series

K. C. Hanson, Charles M. Collier, and D. Christopher Spinks,
Series Editors

Recent volumes in the series:

Poul F. Guttesen
Leaning into the Future

T. David Beck
The Holy Spirit and the Renewal of All Things

Ryan A. Neal
Theology as Hope

Abraham Kunnuthara
Schleiermacher on Christian Consciousness of God's Work in History

Paul S. Chung
Martin Luther and Buddhism

Philip Ruge-Jones
Cross in Tensions

John A. Vissers
The Neo-Orthodox Theology of W. W. Bryden

Stephen Finlan and Vladimir Kharlamov, editors
Theosis: Deification in Christian Theology

Following Jesus in Invaded Space

Doing Theology on Aboriginal Land

CHRIS BUDDEN

☙PICKWICK *Publications* · Eugene, Oregon

FOLLOWING JESUS IN INVADED SPACE
Doing Theology on Aboriginal Land

Princeton Theological Monograph Series 116

Pickwick Publications
A Division of Wipf and Stock Publishers
199 W. 8th Ave., Suite 3
Eugene, OR 97401

ISBN 13: 978-1-60608-608-7

Cataloging-in-Publication data:

Budden, Chris.

Following Jesus in invaded space : doing theology on aboriginal land / Chris Budden.

x + 180 p. ; 23 cm. Includes bibliographical references.

Princeton Theological Monograph Series 116

ISBN 13: 978-1-55635-513-4

1. Christianity and culture. 2. Christianity—Australia. 3. Theology—Australia. I. Title. II. Series.

CALL NUMBER 2009

Manufactured in the U.S.A.

The Scripture quotations are from the New Revised Standard Version Bible, copyright 1989 by the Division of Christian Education of the National Council of the Churches of Christ in the U.S.A.

Grateful acknowledgment is made to the following:

The World Council of Churches, Geneva, for quote from *The Nature and Purpose of the Church: A stage on the way to a common statement* (Faith and Order Paper No. 181, 1998). Used with permission.

The Assembly of the Uniting Church in Sydney, Australia, for permission to draw ideas and quotes from *Theological Foundations for a Covenant as an Expression of the relationship between the UAICC and other parts of the Uniting Church*, by Chris Budden and John Rickard, April 2006.

To the members of
the Uniting Aboriginal and Islander Christian Congress
and Wendy

Contents

Acknowledgments

THIS BOOK ATTEMPTS TO CHART RELATIVELY NEW WATERS. HOWEVER, as the footnotes and bibliography indicate, it is not entirely a new journey. I am indebted to others who have sought to construct an Australian theology, to those who have taught me much about theological method, and to those of my friends and colleagues who have believed in this book and have encouraged me enormously. In particular I am indebted to one of my earliest teachers, Alan Loy, and to Clive Pearson, who has been a good friend, teacher, and colleague as I have explored issues of contextual and public theology. Anthony G. Reddie helped me to be clear that this was a contextualized white theology, and not some attempt to claim another people's story. I am indebted to Stephen Burns, John Brown, and John Rickard who read and commented on earlier drafts. The remaining errors and weaknesses are, of course, mine.

I am grateful to the Hunter Presbytery of the Uniting Church for a scholarship that allowed me to spend two clear months working on the final stages of this work. My congregation, the North Lake Macquarie Uniting Church, has been gracious and supportive in allowing me the leave to write, and for putting up with me while I was sometimes distracted by the constant haunting idea of this book. They are great people and I am grateful to be their minister. Ian and Beth Travis gave me a place to write during my two months' leave, and I will always be grateful for their generosity.

I have dedicated this book to two peoples: first, to the members of the Uniting Aboriginal and Islander Christian Congress who have been my friends, and who have challenged me constantly to confront my presuppositions and way of seeing the world. They have been more gracious than I have deserved. Second, to my wonderful wife, Wendy, who has patiently put up with me as I have labored over this book, often robbed of my time and attention. I am very grateful for her place in my life and journey, and for what she teaches me of relationships, love, and new beginnings.

Introduction

The Task and Its Difficulties

RECENTLY IN SYDNEY, AUSTRALIA, THERE WAS A REPORT OF AN AIR crash involving two small planes. All reference to the male pilot omitted any reference to his gender, while references to the other pilot said "female pilot." This could be repeated in many situations, with "female" being replaced by "black," "Middle Eastern," "Muslim" or other descriptors irrelevant to the situation. The point is that "white" and "male" are considered to be normal and usual, while all else is different.

This book is concerned for what is accepted as normal in social analysis and theology in Australia, with particular reference to Indigenous people and the invasion of this country. It explores the way we defend interests—personal, social, political and economic—through our descriptions of the world and our theology, the way we define frontiers, and how we deal with people on those frontiers. It is concerned for what it means to be part of that people who are Second peoples, invaders and newcomers, and how faith must be approached differently if we are conscious of our place in this land.

I am a fifth-generation white Australian male. My family on my paternal grandfather's side arrived in 1839 on assisted passage as farm laborers. Other parts of the family came more recently, and still other parts reveal little of their history and roots. What they had in common was that they were poor, lower-middle-class families who worked the land and lived in relative isolation in the rural areas of this country. They either actively or passively participated in the imposition of British rule and society onto this land that was inhabited by Indigenous people. Those who came early played a role in the dispossession of Indigenous people, the taking of their land, and their removal to the edges of society.

In all my growing up I heard no references to the people, the particular people, who once occupied the land on which I lived. I just

I

accepted without question that the land that provided my early security and stability was "our land." Nor were questions raised in the church I attended from an early age. Nowhere in worship, Sunday school, or youth group did I hear about Indigenous people or see a church reflecting on its life in this place.[1] My awakening has been a slow one. Years spent building friendships, revisiting my theological roots, facing the racism that seeps into one's soul in this land, and taking tentative steps for justice have brought me to the place where I needed to write this book. This is an attempt to do theology as a white person whose family history has located him as an uninvited guest on Indigenous land in Australia. It is a faltering step towards a contextual theology that takes seriously a history of invasion, dispossession, massacre, racism and continuing disadvantage, and the way that the dominant society (including the church) explained and justified that history and the world that was built after invasion.

Contextual Theology

This is an attempt at contextual, cross-cultural theology. It recognizes that theology is always and necessarily contextual and suggests that those who have been in control of the theological agenda (largely white males) have usually forgotten this, claiming their reality as universal and excluding all other voices. I share Stephen Bevans's understanding of contextual theology as "taking *two* things seriously: the experience of the *past* (recorded in scripture and preserved and defended in tradition) and the experience of the *present*, that is, *context* (individual and social experience, secular or religious culture, social location, and social change)."[2]

Neil Darragh reminds us that contextual theology does not begin with some sort of clean slate. We are already immersed in a theological tradition, and our concern is the reinterpretation of all that we have inherited in the light of a self-conscious awareness of our context.[3] The task of contextual theology is always circular—we move back and forth,

---

1. Only recently have I read an account of the history of relationships between Indigenous and Second peoples in my local area. See Blyton et al., *Wannin Thanbarran*.

2. Bevans, *Models of Contextual Theology*, xvi.

3. Darragh, *Doing Theology Ourselves*, 30.

reading context in the light of the gospel and reading the gospel from the perspective of people's particular location and experience. It is not a question of determining the tradition and then working out how it works contextually, as if the tradition just "is," but of reading the tradition from the perspective of the context. This applies also to the questions one asks, and the framework for the exploration.

Theology that is consciously contextual and that seeks to hear the voice and experience of people who are not always heard will question the way we have read the tradition, the assumptions that people take to that task, and suggest that the tradition is incomplete. It will suggest that the tradition has been constructed by a particular part of the population to meet and pass on their experiences of the journey but does not take account of people who have found themselves in a different relationship with the Christian faith and its practices. The goal of such theology is not simply to describe "reality" but to enable and encourage a more just, liberated, holistic world that reflects the Triune God's intention for the whole of creation.

The theology in this book takes seriously the struggles and questions posed by people in this situation, and seeks to give heed to what they say about their experience of God. The voices that I am seeking to privilege in this account of Second Peoples' theology are the voices of Indigenous people—both those who are present and those from the past. It is theology that consciously and critically reads the theological tradition from the perspective of a person who lives in this land. It recognizes that there is no uncultured *us*, for whom the God revealed in Jesus Christ is always the same across time and place, and it asks what our theological claims mean for *us* today.

Contextual theology draws carefully on a number of conversation partners.[4] The crucial issue is whom one listens to, whose voices we trust, and who we privilege in our conversations. One important and unchanging foundation of this book was the choice to read from within a liberating context in which I privilege the voice of those on the margin, and where I read with suspicion the voice of those in power. I have given particular weight to the voices of Indigenous Australian

---

4. Clive Pearson speaks about conversation partners or textual foils and allies in "Cross-Cultural Theologies in Australia. In Search of Conversation Partners," in Pearson, *Faith in a Hyphen*, 186.

people and theologians, and black, Asian, Latin American, and feminist theologians.

In its own particular way, this book is an attempt to explore faith and identity as a hyphenated reality. The hyphen, though, is very different from what has generally been part of theology, such as Tongan-Australian, Korean-Australian, or Korean-American.[5] This is not about my dual identity in two ethnic cultures, but my identity within colonial invasion: Anglo Australian—on Indigenous, invaded space. My concern is to explore the way the hyphen makes identity and theological expression more open and contestable.

Among our multiple identities (women/men, young/old, gay/straight, migrant, refugee, second-generation), there is one that is essential for theology in the Australian continent. Second people are a people who live on another's "land," not as guests but invaders. We must reflect on humanity, church, and salvation in Christ in the light of a very broken relationship with Indigenous people. I am seeking to explore theology with a suspicion of colonial telling, an awareness of the ambiguity of the good news for a colonized people, and a sense that theology has to do with real socio-political issues and not simply with spiritual realities. I am seeking to do theology in the face of the claim of Indigenous people that they are in this place because of the sovereign purposes of God, that they are made in the image of God, and that they knew God before the invaders brought the gospel.

Any effort to confront the history of colonial invasion and racism in this country will challenge our lives at the deepest level of identity and bodily practice. It is to walk a very fine line between the need to write theology out of a deep encounter with Indigenous experience and the need to be responsible for this theology as a form of self-examination (and not to simply to put the burden on Indigenous people or to use them as an arena for my work). We cannot confront our fear and guilt in solitude and isolation from Indigenous people, yet neither can we ask Indigenous people to do the work of facing racism that belongs to me and others like me. It is also to recognize that theology that seeks to face racism must encounter not just text and story (as important as

5. There has been wonderful work done in Australia in recent years on the whole issue of theology that emerges from Diaspora, from hyphenated identity, and the cross cultural struggle. It has largely been from recent immigrant people seeking to find a new identity in a multicultural Australia. See, particularly, Pearson, ed., *Faith in a Hyphen*.

they are), but real people in their anger and pain. It is to confront what invasion and racism has done to people's bodies, to their way of being in society, and to what Indigenous bodies mean in terms of fear and guilt in European society. As James W. Perkinson says in a different context: "What is required in place of denial is continuous self-confrontation, slow exorcism, and careful revision in a conscious resolve to live 'race' differently. It is ultimately a matter of learning to live creatively out of one's own diverse genealogy and experiment with one's sense of embodiment gracefully—*against* the dominating structures and conforming powers of white supremacy that have already conscripted one's body for their service."[6]

When I began this book, I explored the possibility that I should call it "white" theology in an attempt to be clear that I was not writing an Indigenous theology or telling of the life and experience of Indigenous people. Yet while there are fine examples of "white" theology[7] that have arisen in other places, the Australian context is different at two levels. First, non-Aboriginal Australian identity is not so shaped by race as it is in the USA or in South Africa, for example, largely because Indigenous people are such a small minority (about 4 percent at present). It is possible for Second people to live most of their lives as if they were the "only people." Second, Australia is a very diverse, multicultural community and "white" does not honour that diversity. For people seeking their own cross-cultural, hyphenated identity, "white" is a dominant and dominating identity, a majority worldview that excludes rather than includes.

In an early, otherwise very helpful conversation, it was suggested that this could be a "settler" theology. Yet such a way of naming the project contradicts its very heart: this is not a settled place but invaded space. This is no peacefully entered land, but entry without invitation, a violent possession and dispossession, as well as the location of invaders in ways that have dis-located Indigenous people.

Over the last couple years of conversation with the Uniting Aboriginal and Islander Christian Congress, the Indigenous community that is part of the Uniting Church in Australia, there has been an increasing tendency to speak of Indigenous people as First Peoples.

6. Perkinson, *White Theology*, 47.
7. For example, Perkinson, *White Theology*.

This means that all those who are not Indigenous peoples are Second peoples. Thus it seemed appropriate that I describe this as a book is about Second peoples' theology. Whatever our internal issues, whatever care we must take that some will not dominate the agenda, our common identity at this point is that we live on Indigenous land[8] as a Second peoples.

Of course it may be argued that the experience of recent immigrants is different from that of those who arrived early within the history of European occupation, and cannot really be described as invasion. There is some truth in this claim, certainly to the extent that the experience of coming to the continent was different for each time and people. Yet all of us have come without invitation, have claimed the right to occupy the land of a sovereign people, have not recognized that sovereignty, and have claimed a welcome that was not offered. To those who say Indigenous people could not offer a meaningful invitation in present day Australia, the response must be that this is part of the tragedy of Invasion.

The Shape of the Conversation

"He asked them, 'What are you arguing about with them?' Someone from the crowd answered him, 'Teacher, I brought my son; he has a spirit that makes him unable to speak . . . and I asked your disciples to cast it out, but they could not do so" (Mark 9:16–18).

In commenting on this passage, Ched Myers makes three claims that are central to the claims of this book.[9] First, he suggests that the discourse of capitalist culture has been internalized in ways that render us blind, deaf, and mute to the practices of power and privilege that

---

8. The use of the word "land" is indicative of one the difficulties that are inherent in this attempt to do contextual theology in this country: the struggle with language and meaning. To call this place "land" is to define it within the discourse of European colonialism. It is a discourse that leads to real estate, economic worth, measured space and ownership. It is a discourse that stands over against the metaphors that mark Indigenous discourse: "mother earth," "place," "country," or "home." There is a need for an ongoing conversation about the right language to use. What is important at this point is that this brief sentence about "land" is intended to convey the sense that theology needs to occur with an awareness, a primary and shaping awareness of colonial occupation and the need to relate to Indigenous people as the First peoples of this place that they describe as "mother-earth."

9. Myers, *Who Will Roll Away the Stone?* 76–110 (chapter 4).

mark our own lives. Second, the reason the disciples could not heal the man from his demons was that they were too possessed by their own demons to release others. Third, hope and the capacity to set ourselves and others free begins when illusion ends, when we face our real history and our real participation in structures of power and abuse. In short, hope begins when we are dis-illusioned.

This book is written on the assumption that the churches in Australia have internalized the values of an invading society and its racist and class-based explanations and justifications of invasion. This has made us, even with the best of intentions, unable to hear and see or speak words that provide justice. We have been caught in the "normalcy" that has been imposed on this place and people. The hope of this book is that it will contribute in some small way to disillusionment. I hope it will be a challenge to what is described and accepted as normal, to the capacity to face our captivity and demons, and to be the church and theological community in different ways. "Historical honesty, if the dominant culture has the courage to practice it, would compel us to admit that our 'prosperity' is predicated upon a legacy characterized as much by racism and greed as by liberty and democracy. But we do not face the shadow side of our own story because we are shame-bound and instead suppress historical contradictions while reciting vicious fictions such as the European 'discovery' of the Americas, thinking them essentially benign."[10] Connected with this is the need to recognize the real pain and suffering in invasion and dispossession. Theology has often sought to too easily and quickly incorporate such things into its worldview and to explain them away, when in fact they should challenge and seek to break open that world.

There is always a question of whether one begins in context or methodology or tradition. I have made the decision to start with the context. Chapter 1 is an account of the social, political, and religious context of invasion and dispossession and of the way these have been construed to disadvantage Indigenous people. It is an account of stolen land, massacres and frontier wars, violence, exclusion at law, deaths in custody, the abuse of labor, the many forms of racism, and present disadvantage. It speaks of the church and its location within this struggle. It is a story of location and re-location, of location and dis-location.

10. Ibid., 98. He is speaking of the invasion of the Americas, but it applies equally to Australia.

Chapter 2 begins with a consideration of the way we construct our world and meaning and then explores the way invasion was explained and justified and the role of the church in constructing such a world. It is about *Terra Nullius*, racism in old forms and new, invisibility, and the denial of history. This is not a detailed account of the relationships that exist in this country but a rather inadequate attempt to highlight the core issues: invasion, dispossession, massacres, loss of traditional culture, racism, marginalization, and continuing disadvantage. Readers can check the bibliography if they wish to explore any issue further.

Chapter 3 explores the task of theology, how that relates to the way we encounter God, and how theology brings together and is shaped by the context and the theological tradition of the church. It speaks of the role played by theology in the construction of social reality, a role generally determined by the church's location and relationship with dominant society.

There are at least two, interrelated dangers in this task. The first is the danger that we describe Indigenous people as victims, as people we can pity and do things for. That is not my intention. I have tried to describe the destructiveness and pain of invasion and dispossession, but I also want to acknowledge the strength of Indigenous people and the extraordinary ways they have confronted this invasion. Second, we must at least ask, and continue to be aware of the question, when we speak of oppression, invasion, and disadvantage, whose perspective and question is being privileged? Is this invasion and oppression as defined by well-meaning Europeans, those seeking to contest the colonial discourse for the sake of solidarity, or is it what is described by Aboriginal people? Have we again defined Aboriginal people in terms of categories privileged by invaders, and in terms of what Europeans have done to the "Other," rather than allowing Aboriginal people to define the experience and outcome from their perspective as subjects rather than objects?

The second section of this book confronts us with four particular challenges to Second peoples' theology. They are challenges to the "white" church's claim to define the church and its faith in this place. They challenge the view that doctrines and practices are determined by one tradition, and that others must find a place in that tradition, rather than together exploring what the tradition says and how it is to be claimed today. Each issue asks that other, usually mute voices be heard in the conversation that is the theology and practices of the church.

Each issue is introduced through a story that calls me and the church to face our place, who we stand with, whose voices are heard, and whose interests are protected. Those issues are:

1. Does God actually matter or make a difference, or is "God" just a name for a distant Being who has left the world to its own devices? Is language about God really meaningful in a world shaped by invasion and dispossession, by the Enlightenment, and by science and economy?

2. What does 'justice' mean in this place, and how is power and control exercised around Indigenous peoples?

3. What are the signs and marks of the church in the face of the challenge that the church cannot truly be church apart from a just relationship with Indigenous people?

4. How are we to understand reconciliation and the demand for covenant and treaty?

Readers will quickly recognizes how many important issues are missing—the relationship between gospel and culture, land rights, and the relationship between Christian faith and Indigenous spirituality, for example. Clearly a book that covered all the issue would be very much bigger than this one. My interest in this initial book is for questions that touch the identity of the church and the shape of its faith, for rethinking the place from which we can reflect on these other major issues. Unless we rethink these core issues, we will continue to respond poorly to the central issue of the relationship between First and Second peoples.

Some Issues That Make This a Difficult Conversation[11]

There are issues that make this attempt at contextual theology a particularly fraught one. I have already spoken of the way we define "land" and have suggested that who we listen to is crucial. This latter point needs further reflection, along with the issues of the accepted framework of discourse, how we refer to First people, the danger that who is Indigenous will be narrowed, and the filtering of experience through postinvasion experience.

11. I have previously engaged some of these issues in "Exploring Contextual Theology in Australia."

Australia was populated by hundreds of communities prior to invasion. There is some debate about whether the First peoples should be called Aboriginal people or Indigenous people, both terms in their capitalized version being names and not descriptors. I have chosen to use both, although I largely use Indigenous peoples, as well the term "First Peoples."

When the church decides to whom it will listen, it needs to be aware that such a decision is also a decision about to whom one will not listen. There is a danger that we will not accept those whom Aboriginal people have appointed to speak on their behalf, or that we will expect people to be able to speak for everyone when they cannot, or that we will listen only to those whom we have known for a long time, and who may tell us what we wish to hear. It is easy to exclude the voice of the angry and the truly radical. It is also easy to ignore the voice of women. It is a temptation to act out of ideological presuppositions and to decide what we should do before we listen to what will always be diverse and complex voices.

When anyone seeks to describe a social reality other than their own, they do so within the available discourse of their language and culture. Stephen Muecke reminds us that Europeans always struggle with the fact that Aboriginal people first appear in our discourse as "them," as the other who is never allowed to be subject.[12] The well-worn tracks of discourse in white society are anthropological, romantic, and racist. The challenge is to recognize how easy it is to fall into this sort of discourse while trying to critique it.

In an essay titled "Would the Real Native Please Sit Down!" Jione Havea suggests some other issues that make this task more difficult. He reminds us that at this point in history there is always so much interaction between cultures, culture is always so fluid and changeable, and culture is not a monolith but is always genuinely "multi," that it is difficult to define what "native" (indeed any) culture is. Who can define the Fijian way, the Tongan way, or the Indigenous Australian way? "What non-native values and concerns have assimilated into, and co-opted, those definitions? What native cultural differences are silenced, ignored, and/or homogenized in order for those definitions to delimit? In whose

---

12. Muecke, *Textual Spaces*, 23.

interests?"[13] And, one might add, who decides, and whose voices are allowed to speak? Havea reminds us that identity and culture cannot be settled in essentialist ways, as if there were some unchangeable core, for culture is too fluid and diverse.

It is normally assumed that Indigenous Australian culture is an oral culture, by which it is meant that is it not a book culture. Havea adds that oral cultures are first and foremost *cultures of relations*. It is relationships that determine stories and how they are told, and stories can change as relationships change.[14] The aim is to sustain and transform relationships, which also change stories. The issue for theology as it seeks to listen to the encounter between cultures and theologies is how the hearing can occur within the priorities of relationships, and how a culture of written texts and rules can be open to change that will sustain the merging relationships.

Conclusion

There is a risk in contextual theology that we have not escaped imperialism but only changed its form. There is the danger that people like me will use the experience of others for my own purposes. I have tried to avoid this, but only readers and, particularly, Indigenous people will know if I have succeeded.

There is also the temptation for the contextual task to still be controlled by the academy. There is an openness to new contexts, new stories, and new content in theology, but is there an openness to new ways of doing theology? Is there still the imperialism of one account of academic rigor, of an insistence that all the possible companions are encountered, that the time spent must largely be with academic resources rather than relationships, conversations, and new ponderings? I have been torn in this writing process, wanting to honor those who have attempted this journey before me, but wary that their journey will overwhelm mine, will misshape it, and draw it towards accepted "standards" rather than being my contextual enterprise. I have not resolved this tension. Just as I was finishing the first draft, I spent four days with Indigenous people in a gathering around theology, worship, and liturgy. I was reminded of

---

13. Havea, "Would the Real Native Please Sit Down!" in Pearson, *Faith in a Hyphen*, 201.

14. Ibid., 203.

how much I still need to hear and understand, and how dangerous it is to be locked into libraries and away from real relationships.

I am not trying to make people feel guilty. Nor do I wish to suggest some idealized past to which we must return. We live in this historic moment, which we did not create, but have inherited—good and bad. The issue for us is how we will follow Jesus in this moment, and how and where we will locate ourselves in relation to Indigenous people and our shared history.

At times I have named issues and suggested resources but have not explored them further. The task before us as Second peoples is a big one, and I have only just scratched the surface. My hope is that other younger and smarter theological minds might be challenged to enter the task, to build relationships and pursue these issues, and to redo all that I have done here.

Context and Theological Method

Introduction to Part One

To describe the context is to name the relationships, beliefs, and practices that mark our life, and the narratives and rituals that construct and justify the world. It is to name who we are and from what place we tell the Christian story. When we describe the context we are constructing and not simply recording our history. Our view of what happened in the past depends on where we are in the present. The questions we ask, the issues we name, the events we see will be shaped by our social location and power.

In this section I want to name the relationship that exists between First and Second peoples, a relationship built on a history of invasion, dispossession, and dis-location, and a present experience of marginalization. I also want to speak of the way in which that history has been explained and justified, and what that does to present relationships.

The church and its theology have the task of telling a story that leads to human wholeness and flourishing. Thus an important issue about context is where wholeness is denied, and what part the church has played in that denial. I want to name the ways in which the church has helped explain and justify history and social experience in this place. I want to name the way we have constructed what is "normal," and by implication, to ask whether such telling about the world will endure the scrutiny of the gospel.

What follows is the story of a people dispossessed; shunted to the edge of society by a history of stolen land, massacre, segregation, assimilation (and stolen children), abuse of the law and imprisonment; and continuing marginalization in health, housing, employment, and education. It is the story of a church that sat with empire and often did its theology more as a servant of the state than of the suffering Christ. It is about the story that justified and justifies the society: *terra nullius* that meant people were not here; racism that made people not people, and invisible; and of the claim of benevolence, superiority, and civilization. It is about the way in which the white world and church saw themselves as normal, and barely thought about the way they assumed others should be like them.

There is a danger that, in seeking to understand history and modern social reality we make people into one mob and see everything in term of one model like the "dispossession-resistance model,"[1] or paint Indigenous people only as victims. It is clear that everyone is not the same, and that there were a great variety of responses across the country. It is also clear that, whereas authors from among Second peoples tend to stress the violence and dispossession, Indigenous authors often stress "the themes of initiative, courage and cultural survival."[2] That is, we need to be careful even when writing a sympathetic history that we do not make it our history in which Indigenous people are victims and passive participants. We should not make even well-intentioned history a colonial act of claiming the past for ourselves.

Yet neither should we forget that, whatever choices Indigenous people made in the face of invasion and dispossession, it *was* in the face of invasion, dispossession, and most importantly, a conflict-ridden context marked by "intersecting and differential power relationships of class, race, culture, economy and the 'complex circuitry of domination.'"[3] I tell the story in the following chapters to remind Second peoples that the present reality for Indigenous people is not always one filled with the choices and opportunities they enjoy, but one shaped by a dominant and oppressive society of which they are a part. It is a world constrained by dispossession, racism, poverty and marginalization; a world that serves the needs of the dominant society, and which the church needs to challenge.

Chapter 1 is the story of invasion and dispossession. Chapter 2 speaks of the social construction of reality, and the way invasion has been fitted into the European world. In chapter 3 I suggest what theology is, and how we might actually go about the task of reflecting theologically in particular contexts. My methodology has been shaped by the context in which I live, just as my reading of the context has already been shaped by my theological assumptions.

1. The term comes from Bob Reece, "Inventing Aborigines," in Chapman and Read, eds., *Terrible Hard Biscuits*, 28.

2. Isabel McBryde, "Perspectives on the Past: An Introduction," in Chapman and Read, eds., *Terrible Hard Biscuits*, 6.

3. Bill Thorpe, "Frontiers of Discourse," 44. Thorpe offers a helpful critique of the foundations of this sort of historical revisionism that over stresses co-operation.

1

The Context

Location and Dis-Location in Indigenous Space

Introduction

THE PRIMARY DEFINING CONTEXT FOR THOSE WHO LIVE IN AUSTRALIA is invasion.[1] Invasion is about land and country, social location, power, place in the world, and meaning. It is about the place of nations in the world. The violence that accompanies invasion is a reminder of the defeated people's place in a new world. Colonial invasion is essentially about the claims of a nation to occupy land that has been the home of indigenous people. It removes people's rights to control of land, economy, political life and religious story, along with language and worldview. Colonial invasion disrupts worlds, and the story that explains the world.

By the very nature of invasion it is land that is the most contested point of the relationship between two people. Land holds and makes meaning. It is social location, economic base, a site for political and civil life, a place for sacred sites and their attending stories. This was as true for the people of Israel, as it was for the British invaders, and as it was for Indigenous people. To be removed from land, to be deprived of access to place, is disruptive in a multitude of ways.

Invasion and colonial expansion has to do with relations at the frontier and at the centre. David Chidester suggests that frontiers are

---

1. The word "invasion" is a disturbing one for most Australians. It carries the image of war and violence. It harshly contradicts the idea that this continent was peacefully settled. However, I agree with Henry Reynolds when he says: "if you arrive without being invited in another country and you bring military force with you with the intention of using the force to impose your will, then 'it has to be interpreted by any measure as an invasion'" (*Why Weren't We Told?* 166).

not lines or boundaries or borders, but "a region of intercultural relations between intrusive and indigenous people."[2] I would suggest that it is at the frontier, at the point where control is most contested that the relationship is most abusive and yet, paradoxically, also the most "co-operative" and possible because the invaders need the indigenous people. In those places where the frontier has been closed—at the point of invader hegemony and the establishment of control—the invader has no need of indigenous people, and they are segregated and pushed to the very margins of life. Now they can be "protected" and converted and made to disappear culturally.

The European invasion of Australia was a violent clash between two complex and sophisticated cultures that was won by the people with most numbers and the greater military strength, a people who had honed their techniques in the stealing of the lands of people in India and the United States.

The Indigenous peoples of Australia were a people whose culture, language, traditions, and ways of living varied between the various clans and tribal groupings. They were a people with complex social and political structures, trade routes across the country and into parts of Asia, who had recognized ways of allowing people onto their land for specific purposes, who cultivated and farmed the land and sea, who were nomadic in some places and quite settled in others, and who lived in simple humpies, or large tree-bark huts, and in large dwellings made of stone, timber, and turf. They stored grains in stone silos, smoked excess eels and stored them for future needs, and tended acres of gardens. They possessed the oldest languages in the world, the first art and dance and, possibly, the first boats.[3] The language that was used to describe the colonial situation—e.g. *terra nullius* (literally "empty and unoccupied"), primitive, and uncivilized—were not factual descriptors but the narra-

2. Chidester, *Savage Systems*, 20.

3. For more details on these claims, readers should turn to the Indigenous authors listed in the bibliography. One particularly good description of the complex culture of the peoples in what is now Victoria and Tasmania is Pascoe, *Convincing Ground*. As he suggests, one of the problems with white knowledge of Indigenous culture is that in the more settled areas, the settlement was destroyed and denied. By the time the anthropologists wrote they spoke only of the people of the north who lived in arid regions where large-scale agriculture was impossible—for anyone (126). We now see this more nomadic culture as the only and real Indigenous culture, and nothing could be further from the truth.

tive used to defend and explain dispossession and violence. This is the language that constructed a world of peaceful settlement, benevolence, and the conversion of "pagans."

The place of Christians and the church in this history was one of ambiguity. It is the story of people who defended Indigenous people with integrity, of missions that both protected and destroyed, and of church leaders who shared the widely held belief that Indigenous people were a primitive community that would give way before superior civilization. It is the story of people who believed that Indigenous people were of One Blood with Europeans and could be brought to faith in Christ, and of people who attended church on Sunday mornings and killed Indigenous people later in the day in order to claim their country.

Invasion and the Imposition of Order

The agenda of the British government was clear and multifaceted—the expansion of British influence and power, stopping the expansion of French influence in this part of the world, finding an alternative place to send prison inmates after the loss of the American colonies, and developing new economic opportunities. The only issue was, how would they deal with the people who were already present in the land?

Invasion is about the imposition of a new order and new sense of meaning on an invaded people and land. It is about both the removal and (often) enslavement of people, and about imposing a new order that will justify this removal and enslavement, and will convince people to accept this order. In Australia this meant locating a people considered (wrongly) to be uncivilized, primitive, pagan, and without rights on the edges of a community that saw itself as the pinnacle of civilized life— white, British, Christian, enlightened, and scientifically sophisticated. At the very least it meant conversion and civilizing (often considered the same thing). To enforce this new set of social relationships involved denial of land and sovereignty, violence, imprisonment, slavelike work, herding people onto missions, and continually changing social policies (assimilation, integration, self-determination) that involved stolen children and denial of separate identity. It was a situation underpinned by racism and paternalism.

Stolen Land

The voyage of Christopher Columbus (1492) greatly expanded Europe's understanding of the world and began a series of voyages that led to European nations' claiming sovereignty over the "new" lands. The constant danger was that the various European powers would interfere with one another's activities, and war would ensue. So the doctrine of "discovery" was developed, which explained the right of nations who "discovered" previously unknown lands and regulated relationships between European nations. Discovery gave a right of sovereignty (the assumption being that the local people were not civilized enough to exercise sovereignty) but did not provide a justification for claiming ownership of the land.

Yet for various reasons, and despite some official policies that recognized Indigenous ownership of land, there was no official attempt to recognize the existence of Indigenous people as owners of their land, to make treaties, or to purchase the land. The relationship between the two peoples began in theft. The European invaders drove people from their land, destroyed their homes and sources of food, denied them access to sacred sites and their connected stories, and in the process undermined the sociality at the heart of identity. Also destroyed was people's capacity to live from the land. The advent of cattle and sheep changed the landscape and made it unproductive for many vital food and medical plants, destroyed waterholes, and robbed the native animals of access to food.

For the Europeans who invaded Australia, land was largely a commodity, a basis for economic activity and productivity. There was no connection between their religious "temples" and stories and any particular piece of land. Land was to be mined, grazed and farmed, sold as real estate, and owned as a source and sign of wealth. It was landscape, something to be viewed from the outside, dissected and explained, portrayed in painting and film. However we would misunderstand history, colonization, and our present struggles over land if we failed to see that land was more than this. The colonizers moved from a place, a story, a home and politics to another place, and sought in their new place economic foundations, founding and sustaining myths, and a home (that both reminded them of and was different from the old home).

What was profoundly different between the invading people and the Indigenous community was that for Indigenous people meaning was tied inexorably and unchangeably to particular land and particular places. Economy and meaning and sacred place could not be shifted, uprooted, or changed. There was an intimate social, religious, and economic connection between people and their particular place. "To Aboriginal people the land was not just soil or rock or minerals, but the whole environment—the land, the water, the air and all the life they supported, including woman and man; all the elements, the sun, the moon, the stars and the sky—all related and linked by the Dreamtime. Humans were not separated from their environment, but indivisibly united with it. Aboriginals were part of the land and it was part of them. When they lost the land they lost themselves."[4]

It is important to understand this intimate relationship between people and land, for it is a two-way thing. It is not just people who are harmed by invasion and dispossession, but the land. The mutuality of care, the way in which the people nurture the land, and are nurtured by it, is threatened. Indigenous people believe that land is not inanimate but has feelings and bears messages and stories. When the people are gone, the country is lonely and sad; it misses the people and their care of the land.[5]

To hear land valued in this spiritual way can be misleading for Second peoples, who are used to a distinction, indeed separation, between the sacred and the secular. But in a world where this distinction does not exist, to speak this way is to "include the role land plays in social relations, political relations, and in the cultural construction and transmission of knowledge."[6] For Indigenous people land was and is an economic resource, it is where religious knowledge is embedded and inscribed, and where relationships are subscribed. It is the source of political standing and authority and the basis for obligation and responsibilities.

The challenge for present relationships and theology is that the land we exist on is stolen land, it is land taken without right, and justified by naked power and foreign laws. Indigenous people have never

4. Parbury, *Survival*, 15–16.

5. For a very good account of this way of understanding land and people see Morgan et al., *Heartsick for Country*.

6. Goodall, *Invasion to Embassy*, 1.

given up the claim that this is their land. Economically and symbolically there has been a never-ending, if changing, struggle for land. It is a struggle that finds a place among other struggles—wages, political rights, deaths in custody, stolen children, health and legal services—but while its priority might change in different situations and contexts, it never goes away. This raises the question of how the church relates to Indigenous people when they occupy and have built their wealth on this land.

Massacres and Frontier Wars

Invasion is by its very nature always accompanied by violence, for invasion is about theft and keeping people in their "right" place. A people for whom land is so central do not simply walk away and allow invaders to take their place. When the First fleet sailed into Port Jackson to establish a convict colony, the Indigenous people were initially friendly, believing that the new arrivals would stay only a short time. Indeed it was incomprehensible within their social and political system that strangers would come and claim the right to occupy what was clearly their land, not empty and unoccupied or unused, but filled with meaning and activity. When they realized that Phillip and his fleet intended to stay permanently, they became hostile, and conflict broke out. This was the beginning of a terrible contest, and of the violence that has marked the frontier in all colonial invasions around the world.[7]

Resistance was met with harsh retaliation. Every state in Australia has massacre sites that haunt the memory of Aboriginal people, some of the massacres having occurred during the last century.[8] Sometimes these massacres occurred just for a lark, sometimes because Indigenous people were considered a bit "uppity" and needed to be taught a lesson, and sometimes in retaliation for the killing of a white person or sheep or cattle. Mostly they were killed because the newcomers understood

7. A fuller discussion of the resistance is found in Broome, *Aboriginal Australians*; Reynolds, *The Other Side of the Frontier* (chapter 3); and *Why Weren't We Told?*, chaps. 10–12; and Pascoe, *Convincing Ground*. We should be careful, of course, that "resistance" does not replace "faded away" as a descriptor of all people, and not fail to understand the quite diverse responses in different places.

8. Details of massacres are found in Parbury, *Survival*, 58–59; Broome, *Aboriginal Australians* (chapter 3); Reynolds, *Why Weren't We Told?*, chaps. 9 and 10; Pascoe, *Convincing* Ground; and Habel, *Reconciliation*.

this to be a serious war, a struggle for place by two people claiming the same "home."

The massacres were consistently denied and the extent of the deaths always underestimated. The historical accounts covered over the extent of the destruction by claiming that there had been only 300,000 Indigenous people in 1788, while the evidence now suggests 750,000 people; reduced to 100,00 by policies of genocide. There is also denial of the frontier wars, of the struggle of Indigenous people against impossible odds to defend their land. The records ignore the fact that more Indigenous Australians were killed in the undeclared frontier wars than Australian soldiers were lost in the Boer War (518), the Korean War (277) and the war in Vietnam (414).

Henry Reynolds makes the case that many of the early colonists recognized that they were involved in a war, and Indigenous people certainly believed that they were. Indigenous people were not simply the helpless victims of massacres but people killed in an ongoing frontier war that often made no distinction between soldiers and other people. This was a war to take ownership of land and to dispossess those who had been here for thousands of years. The idea that there was a war is denied because to acknowledge war is to face the moral issue of dispossession from the land of a defeated people with whom there should be a recognition of sovereignty and a treaty.[9]

Violence and Mistreatment

Indigenous people have experienced an enormous amount of violence in Australia, much of it unrecorded but still part of people's memory. The official part is seen in imprisonment and deaths in custody, but it is found in police brutality, communal violence, and mistreatment by employers in isolated places.

For example, as the pastoral industry expanded across Queensland, the Northern Territory, and Western Australia, and as people tried to stay on their land or sought work, there developed the sort of harsh violence that marks social frontiers. They are ambiguous places filled with mutual need and respect, physical and sexual abuse, humiliation, and control whose purpose was to keep people in their place (maybe because the other social boundaries did not exist).

9. Reynolds, *Why Weren't We Told?* (chapter 12).

In an early feminist interpretation of Australian colonial history, Anne Summers developed the thesis that women in Australia were stereotyped as "damned whores or God's police."[10] While the tag of "whore" was first attached to female convicts, so strong was the idea that other women were labeled the same way. Indigenous women were quickly lumped into that category and treated as women to have sex with but never to marry or share life with. Anne Pattel-Gray details the abuse suffered by women—repeated assault, pack rape, enslavement, genital mutilation, and, often, murder—and the way white women closed their eyes to this abuse rather than harm their Victorian sensibilities.[11] The people around Victor Harbor in South Australia, for example, still relate the stories of their women being taken by whalers, many dropped from their boats a considerable distance away (even as far as Tasmania) or simply killed. The stories of abuse, murder, and loss of family remain painfully in people's memories.

Excluded at Law

Even when Indigenous people were recognized as human beings, the issue was: what rights did they have before the law? Implicitly the question was, are they to be treated as equal citizens? The answer was clearly no. Their oath was unacceptable in court, their murderers were usually not tried, but Indigenous people were hunted ruthlessly without regard for the law if they killed a white person. By 1840 Indigenous people in New South Wales could be arrested and held without trial, were unable to testify before a court, and could not buy alcohol or carry a gun.[12] They were not counted as Australian citizens until 1967, and those few who could vote prior to 1901 were disenfranchised at federation. They could not marry unless they proved that they could live almost like a white person.[13]

In a situation anticipating South African apartheid, laws such as the 1851 Vagrancy Act in New South Wales prohibited blacks and whites from cohabitating. Schools were segregated, with Aboriginal children

10. Summers, *Damned Whores and God's Police*.

11. Pattel-Gray, *The Great White Flood*, 167–68.

12. Broome, *Aboriginal Australians*, 95.

13. For a more personalized account of this sort of experience, see Dingo, *The Story of Our Mob*, 134.

being given untrained teachers, usually the wife of the manager of the reserve on which they lived. Children could be banned from school right through to the 1960s in New South Wales if a white parent complained about their presence. Men could fight for their country during war, but unless they had what was called a dog tag, proof that they were almost white, they couldn't drink in a pub. "Wherever they were ... most Aborigines came under special acts, were denied civil rights, and felt the cold chill of white prejudice. By the early twentieth century, racism not only permeated the community, but was enshrined in its acts which treated Aboriginal people as different and inferior."[14]

Imprisonment and Deaths in Custody

Peggy Brock argues, as I have done, that the essential relationship in Australia has been one of containing and controlling Indigenous people, although the method of control changed at different times. Her thesis is that police and missions were used to implement government policies, and that intervention was most active when Indigenous people were most present in society.[15] She argues that in South Australia, for example, imprisonment rates were high in the 1850s and 60s during the time of imposition of colonial rule and dispossession. They were then low toward the end of the nineteenth century, when dispossession was achieved, and Indigenous people were largely neglected. The rates remained low in the first thirty years of the twentieth century, largely because of a policy of segregation that was overseen by another set of institutions (including the church). From the 1950s and the development of assimilation policies, we have a period marked by high rates of arrest and incarceration, which "suggests that the criminal justice system is once again being used as a tool to subject indigenous people to government control."[16] It is worth remembering that during the time of segregation, which was often justified as a period of "protection," there were a range of activities that were illegal for Aboriginal people but legal for other citizens—moving freely, drinking alcohol, controlling earnings, controlling children. Breach of these discriminatory laws

14. Broome, *Aboriginal Australians*, 104.
15. Brock, "Protecting Colonial Interests."
16. Ibid., 127–28.

was one of the most frequent causes of entry into the criminal justice system.

Indigenous people are still overrepresented in the prison system; for example, in 2003 20 percent of prisoners in Australian jails identified as Indigenous. In 1998, Indigenous men were imprisoned at a rate of 3,218.8 per 100,000 whilst non-Indigenous men were imprisoned at a rate of 216.98 per 100,000. In the same year Indigenous women were eighteen times more likely to be imprisoned than non-Indigenous women. Indigenous people are not in prison in greater numbers because they are more criminal by nature. Prison rates depend on how crime is defined for any group, on the extent of policing for any group, on the way the court sentences people for the same crimes, on what people need to do to survive, and on where anger gets directed when there is no meaning in life. The statistics clearly show that Aboriginal people have always been overrepresented in the criminal justice system, not because they are more likely to commit a crime, but because they are more likely to be arrested and to serve time for a minor crime than a white person is. Indigenous people also frequently receive harsher penalties than other Australians for the same crime.

The Royal Commission into Aboriginal Deaths in Custody (1988) made it clear that the number of Aboriginal deaths in custody is a significant tragedy. Indigenous deaths occur at a far greater rate than deaths of other Australians, and the level of care for incarcerated people is quite inadequate. The high level of imprisonment of Indigenous people has not improved since the Royal Commission. Indeed, matters have gotten worse.[17] Those who are most oppressed and marginalized, those who are meant to be silent and invisible are criminalized by their colored presence on the streets. They are criminals because they are Indigenous people. The nature of racism in this country makes Indigenous people the dangerous "other," to be feared and criminalized and, paradoxically, ignored.

---

17. For further details see, for example, Cunneen, *Review of Indigenous Deaths in Custody*; the Australian Institute of Criminology, "Crime Facts Info No. 88"; and "Indigenous Justice in Australia"; Krieg. "Aboriginal incarceration"; Grant, "Imprisonment of Indigenous Women in Australia 1988–1998" <http://reconciliation.org.au/nsw/education-kit/about/>, which offers a good account of the issues and points to some excellent references; see also Healey, *Indigenous Australians and the Law*; Broome, *Aboriginal Australians*, 220–24.

The Abuse of Labor

There was one area of life where Indigenous people were allowed to be present, even if they remained socially invisible—cheap labor. The new colonial economy needed cheap labor, and once convicts were no longer transported to Australia, Indigenous people were a necessary source of that labor. In some areas, Indigenous people provided such an important source of cheap farm labor that successful black farms were forcibly closed because local white farmers could not get cheap labor while these farms succeeded.[18] For most of this time Indigenous workers received a fraction of the wages paid to other workers, and it was well into the twentieth century until Indigenous people received equal pay for equal work.

A good example of this mistreatment of Indigenous people is found in the pastoral industry, which could not have developed without Aboriginal people. They were at the whim of station managers about access to work, where they could live, and the way they were treated. Sometimes people stayed and worked on stations to be near their country. Sometimes they really enjoyed the work and would move around the stations earning their living, the women working as maids and child-minders in the 'big house.' Indigenous people were rarely paid, existing on rations and living rough, always living a precarious existence dictated by the station managers.[19]

As Anne Pattel-Gray says: "Thus, Aboriginal People were given no rights at all and, quite the contrary, were literally enslaved. While the actual word 'slavery' was not used very often (at least not by whites), the actual practice was basically a white-initiated slave economy based on the forced labours of the Aboriginal People and of the imported European convicts."[20] She goes on to make the claim that Aboriginal

18. This occurred at Singleton in New South Wales, for example. See Miller, *Koori*, 125.

19. For an insightful account of the relationship in the pastoral industry from an Indigenous people's perspective see Dingo, *Dingo*. For an account of the way colonists in Western Australia between 1828 and 1850 (when convicts first arrived there) sought Indigenous people (both adults and children) as a cheap source of labor, see Hetherington, "Aboriginal Children as a Potential Labour Force."

20. Pattel-Gray, *Great White Flood*, 19. Miller has an account of the way white people depended on Indigenous labor in the 1850s because of the shortage of labor caused by the gold rush. Miller tells how the skills and perseverance of Indigenous people were well regarded but that never were they paid a proper wage (Miller, *Koori*, 67).

people were kidnapped, enslaved, and forced into service by many colonists, including police, clergy, and rich individuals.[21]

Segregation, Assimilation and Integration

Australia was to be a white society, and the existence of Indigenous people was a constant anomaly that was dealt with by violence, segregation, and assimilation underpinned by racism and paternalism. The struggle was always what to do with Indigenous people and how to make them invisible. The policies—segregation, assimilation, integration, and self-determination—are all about making Indigenous people disappear as a separate people, absorbed completely into mainstream society.

When Indigenous people couldn't be seen they were ignored. When they moved nearer to white communities there was a forced invisibility. They were required by law to be out of town by sunset, and made to live in shantytowns away from the other towns. When it was believed that they would die out, missions were established to make the dying easier.[22] Indigenous people were segregated on church missions (often reflecting the ambivalent policies of care, conversion, civilization, and keeping people away from white society) and on other "missions." When it became clear that people would not die out, the policy became one of assimilation. At the beginning of the twentieth century, legislation was enacted in a number of states to "protect" Indigenous people, and to provide the situation in which they could learn what politicians believed were the necessary skills to be assimilated into European society. While Indigenous people might continue to exist genetically, they would cease to exist in any ethnological sense.

One of the cruelest parts of the assimilation policy was the decision to take children from their parents if one of those parents was white. The belief was that if they could be removed from the influence of Indigenous families, they had a chance to assimilate into white society (even if, as the process showed, it was to be as servants and other members of the lower working class). This was the people who would become the stolen generation. "The term 'stolen generations' refers to

21. Pattel-Gray, *Great White Flood*, 22.

22. Of course the churches did not generally establish the missions just for this purpose. Missionaries were often genuinely concerned for the welfare of Aboriginal people, and many committed a large part of their lives to serving among Indigenous communities.

Aboriginal and Torres Strait Islander Australians who were forcibly re-moved from their families and communities by government, welfare or church authorities as children and placed into institutional care or with non-Indigenous foster families. The forced removal of Aboriginal and Torres Strait Islander children began as early as the mid 1800s and con-tinued until 1970."[23] Indeed there is evidence of children taken as early as 1824 at Wellington in New South Wales. "Stolen generations" also refers to the generations who are descended from these stolen children and who, as a result, were separated from their heritage and culture.

The Federal Human Rights and Equal Opportunities Commission conducted an enquiry in 1997 into the separation of Indigenous people from their families. Their report, *Bringing Them Home*, contains many stories and much evidence of this painful chapter in Australian history. While it is true that some children were removed for genuine welfare reasons, and some removed children did gain the advantage of a bet-ter education, the overall impact of removal was damaging—the loss of family, relationships, and identity. It was a policy based on the racist as-sumption the "full bloods" would be left to die out, but those with "white blood" might change and become part of the wider society.[24]

In the 1970s the government moved to what was described as a policy of self-determination. In reality it was a policy of limited self-management within government-established goals and guidelines. It was about limited rights in a framework of paternalism and racism.

The Church and Its Location in This Struggle[25]

Where the church locates itself in the social and political world will significantly shape the way it celebrates and tells the gospel story. To understand the theology of the Australian church and the struggle we face to do contextual theology as Second peoples, we need to remember

23. Reconciliation Australia, "Apology to the Stolen Generations."

24. For a full account of the Stolen Generation see *Bringing Them Home*, the report of the Human Rights and Equal Opportunities Commission. For a helpful account of the process involved and some of the responses to the report, see Buti, *Sir Ronald Wilson*, 301–76.

25. This is an account of the church within the Reformed tradition, to which the Uniting Church belongs. For an account of the response of the Roman Catholic Church to Indigenous people, see O'Sullivan, *Faith, Politics and Reconciliation*.

were we have been located in the colonizing society. We need to name the interests we protect.

At each stage of the relationship with Indigenous people—destruction and massacre (and the hope/ belief that they would die out before a superior "civilization"), segregation, and assimilation (and the hope that people would cease to be Aboriginal in any meaningful way), the church played a role.[26] The churches played a very ambiguous role in invasion and the establishment of the frontiers and control. Located as they were (except for the Roman Catholic Church) at the centre of colonial society, and convinced that being human meant being converted to the Christian faith and civilized in the British way, the church remained largely silent in the face of the treatment of Indigenous people, or cooperated with Government policy.

The power of the church is in its ownership of property, its wealth, its traditional influence and, most crucially, the role it plays as temple. That is, the church's place and influence in society is determined not by its coercive power but by the fact that it tells and celebrates the metanarrative, the overarching world-view that explains and justifies life within a culture. Even if the church's control of the major explanatory narrative was being lessened by the narrative of the Enlightenment, it was still a dominant account of life. Those who stole land and killed people—both acts which contradict the Christian faith—needed to find reasons for their actions that would fit within that story. This usually meant the denial of people's humanity and place in God's purpose. Of course the church is also constantly under pressure to interpret its story in ways that reflect and fit in with the dominant political, economic and social agendas of the day. The story of invasion in Australia reflects both tendencies.

A major difficulty for the church in Australia was that the world had moved. This was now an Enlightenment world dominated by human reason, scientific knowledge, and a God who was seen as akin to the absent clock-maker. Australia was a world dominated by fate rather than providence, and religious life was about recognition of a God who set moral rules and social order but was little involved in

26. The role of the church is far too complex and detailed to be laid out in full in this section. For more detail see Broome, *Aboriginal Australians* (chapter 7); Pattel-Gray, *Great White Flood* (chapter 5); Miller, *Koori* (chapter 8). For a sympathetic account see Harris, *One Blood*.

daily life. This was a God who needed to be taken to new places in the church's rituals, stories, institutions and inner religious life. It was a world divided between the private and the public, between Sunday and the rest of the week.

In Australia the power of the church was more limited in all ways than it was in Great Britain. The decreased power of the church, and the growth of a broader culture in which language about God was more difficult and less readily accepted, often led the church to accept the role of agents of government in social control, care of women and children and the aged, and protector of social stability. In regard to Indigenous people this meant becoming official protectors, running missions, co-operating in the "care" of the stolen generation, and often remaining silent in the face of abuse.

This was a church that had trouble defining itself as church apart from its relationship with, and role alongside the government and other leaders in society. It located itself within a settler society, always on the edge of this community that had serious questions about God and providence and cosmic order, becoming a moral policeman rather than teller of meaning and, far too often, a servant of government policy. As a people who sit in that place it has rarely sought to reflect on what the gospel means in this place of conquest and marginalization of Indigenous people. This meant that the church largely stayed silent in the face of racism, racist practices, and the abuse from settler society, governments, and the scientific community that was aimed at removal and destruction. It did try to argue for the humanity of Indigenous people, although leading churchmen like Bishop Broughton did tell the Select Committee on Aborigines in 1837 that Aboriginal people just seemed to decay and vanish in the face of European society.[27] At worst it remained silent in the face of abuse and murder, and reinforced the view that it was alright to take Indigenous land (because they had not used it productively as God had intended).

The churches ran institutions to train young people who would become part of society as largely servant members of the lower classes, and opened mission stations in the more remote areas from the early parts of the Twentieth century. Miller says that some Indigenous people actually described these missions as being like a concentration camp.

27. Pascoe, *Convincing Ground*, 38.

People were removed from traditional areas and rounded up into the camps, their movement was restricted, they were used as a source of cheap labor, received only a few rations, and were indoctrinated in the ways of white people (while not being able to fraternize socially with white people, or live in towns).[28] The church played a role in segregation, the institutionalization of children (both in dormitories on missions and co-operation in the taking of children), and the teaching of the so-called civilized values of European society (including obedience, industry and order).

The only debate was whether the church was actually doing this to "protect" Indigenous people or was simply serving the agenda of those who wished to separate Indigenous people from their land and from other people. Broome believes that all sorts of motives existed in the formation of missions. They were about conversion, civilization, control, change of culture, all under the guise of a paternalism that treated Indigenous people like children. The Missionaries were a mixture of the enlightened, the open, the caring, the violent, and the racist. Nearly all of them, even with the best intention in the world, were paternalistic and convinced that Indigenous people needed to be civilized.[29]

The church rarely—dare one say never—related to Indigenous people as equal human beings, with equal rights, a valuable and complex culture, and an understanding of God. In reality it could be no other way. The church was convinced that Indigenous people needed to be brought to faith in Jesus Christ. Contact with Indigenous people would always be a frontier place in Chidester's sense, a place of conflict between different views of religion, faith, morality and God. As Pattel-Gray says, the church "had vested interests in the religio-political drama being played out in the colonial enterprise. Australian church theology always has been caught in the trap of justifying the ferocious colonization machinery that protected and defended its very existence in this colony, through its similarly—but certainly not admittedly—ferocious missionization policies and practices."[30] She makes the challenging judgment that: "The Australian church, in its activities and teachings, continually contradicted the liberating truth

---

28. Miller, *Koori*, 99.

29. Broome, *Aboriginal Australians* (chapter 7).

30. Pattel-Gray, *Great White Flood*, 122.

of Jesus Christ. It refused to speak the truth in the face of dispossession, massacres, cultural genocide, physical and mental tortures of many kinds, and more…[it] propagated and implemented a theology that was heretical, as it did not search for the ultimate truth but rather stopped short in the netherworld of racism, genocide and oppression against Australian Aboriginal People."[31]

From the perspective of this book, a significant issue is that the church, the major holder of ultimate narrative, could find no place for the religious and social claims of Indigenous people. There was little sense that this was a people made in the image of God who could not then be made in the image of white people. There was no sense that this people may have been put on this land by God, or that this people already had some sense of God. There was none of the respect needed to treat Indigenous people as real neighbors, as the "other" whom the church needed to serve justly. The history of the relationship between the church and Indigenous people has largely been one of paternalism, racism, lack of respect, and an unwillingness to treat Indigenous people as part of the church (rather than an issue for the church). It is a harsh judgment and one difficult to hear, but it is one that even Indigenous Christians make of the church.

There were two factors that contributed to this way the church responded to invasion, dispossession and continuing marginalization: the church's relationship to the state, and its attitude to those who were poor (because of its place in the middle and upper classes)

The Social Location of the Church in Relation to the State.

The church in Australia entered the colony as a partner with the colonial government, even if it was a partnership that was viewed with some skepticism at times. The particular social location of the church in Australia had been shaped by Christendom and its gradual demise, and the emergence of the modern nation state and industrialization.[32]

Despite the early church's clear political affirmation that "Jesus is Lord" (and, thus, the Emperor is not), and its struggle to hold to the priority of discipleship rather than citizenship, this changed over time.

---

31. Ibid., 121.

32. I have explored these issues in more detail in "The Location of God," and "Discipleship and Citizenship."

After the conversion of the Emperor Constantine in the fourth century the church slowly moved to the centre of social and political power. Its role was to legitimate the structures and power of society. It provided the religious guarantee that how things were, was the ways things should be. By the time of the Middle Ages there was no distinction between Church and society and, indeed, the church was the total society. As Davis says: "In such a system the political community is identical with the religious community in theory and substantially so in fact, the religious ideas of the community legitimate the power structure and the religiously integrated and legitimated social system, not an efficient government apparatus, is the chief means of social control."[33]

Christendom collapsed for a variety of reasons, significant among them being the emergence of the modern nation state. One of the needs of the emerging nation state after the time of the Reformation was to establish itself as the body which could demand absolute allegiance from all citizens. All things exist within the nation. People's principal loyalty is to the state, which in return provides protection and security. This meant that religion and discipleship needed to be reframed as a personal and private matter, and people had to see that citizenship and discipleship were essentially the same things. The church became a voluntary association, and faith largely existed in the private sphere. The church is allowed a place within this reality to support citizenship, and the existence of the democratic state, and to provide private morality. The church became the holder of the narrative that sustained the life of the community, and the sanctity of the state. If citizenship and discipleship are co-extensive, it is citizenship which determines values and priorities. The church saw itself as an obedient servant of the state or, at its most critical, a loyal opposition.

At the time of the invasion of Australia the church was still seen as the holder of the major explanatory meta-narrative, and the conductor of the liturgical events which marked the life of the society (even if this role was increasingly contested). It was still seen as the moral guardian of society (at least by the middle classes). Its sense of identity and well-being were tied to a close relationship with those in power.

33. Davis, *Theology and Political Society*, 33.

The Social Location of the Church in Relation to the Poor

In England, with some minor and occasional exceptions, the church leadership was found among the upper classes, and the values of the church were largely those of that leadership. Andre Bieler makes the point that, as the Industrial Revolution occurred in Europe from the 1750s, the churches did little to understand the huge human struggles that were involved in changes in work, family structures, urbanization, the distribution of wealth, colonialization, and supporting ideologies. Generally the churches remained (and remain) largely preindustrial in their theology and outlook. The church didn't loose touch with the working class, for largely it never made contact with this group of people who emerged painfully from the Industrial revolution.[34] The natural location of the churches was the old aristocracy, and the newly emerging middle-classes.

While a very small number of churches sought to build connections with the emerging working class and their issues and struggles, the most that even a caring church could do was get involved in acts of charity. Care for the poor was possible as long as it didn't challenge the structures of society, and the essential relationships of power and economy.

The guiding world-view of the industrial middle-classes was economic and political liberalism. A combination of the Enlightenment philosophy of human freedom and equality, and the puritan ethic that was a mark of Protestantism, this world-view was important in the overthrow of the old political regimes. For example, the middle classes combined with the more radical parts of the working class movement to obtain the Electoral Reform Act of 1832, "which, by widening the electorate, began the end of the supremacy of the landed gentry, but merely in favor of the middle classes".[35] Interesting in terms of our concern for the social location of the churches, the Church of England opposed these electoral reforms.

What this means is that the church in its social location was almost always on the wrong side of the frontier. We accepted as normal the priority of citizenship and support for the nation, the benevolence of empire, the class structure of society and our place in the middle class,

34. Bieler, "Gradual Awareness of Social, Economic Problems (1750–1900)," 7.
35. Ibid., 22.

and the normalcy of "whiteness." As a result the church stood almost without thought with those who wanted to turn frontier into conquered world, who imposed their order on life, sometimes with concern for people's welfare but never with questions about the basic claims. It failed to understand that the theological frontier, the place where one might encounter God, was where Indigenous people were treated justly in relationships as a genuinely valuable "other." It too often chose location with empire over location with Christ among the very least of the brothers and sisters.

The Present Reality

Invasion and a history of racism and dispossession continue to contribute to the marginalization of Indigenous peoples. In the areas of education, health, housing, employment, disposable income, justice, and family stress, Indigenous people are significantly worse off than the population in general. (In the figures which follow the figures in square brackets are those of the general population).

Education:

- Only 32 percent of the Indigenous population have a postschool qualification [57 percent for non-Indigenous people].

- The Indigenous population comprises only one percent of all higher education students.

- Retention ratios: Year 9—97.8 percent for Indigenous people [99.8 percent for non-Indigenous], Year 10—86.4 [98.5 percent for non-Indigenous]; Year 11—58.9 percent for Indigenous people [88.7 percent for non-Indigenous], Year 12—38.0 [76.3 percent].

- Only 3.7 percent have a bachelor's degree [16.9 percent of non-Indigenous people], and 24.1 percent a certificate or diploma [32.7 of non-Indigenous people].

Health:

- Indigenous Australians experience an earlier onset of most chronic diseases, and their rate of diabetes is four times greater than non-Indigenous Australians.

- Indigenous people are twelve times more like to be hospitalized, and they have a greater need for general-practitioner consultations.

Housing:

- Where there are Indigenous people in a household their housing situation is: renting, 63.5 percent [26.6 percent of non-Indigenous people]; purchasing, 19.4 percent [27.0 percent of non-Indigenous people]; owning, 12.6 percent [40.5 percent of non-Indigenous people]; not known, 4.5 percent [5.9 percent of non-Indigenous people].

Employment:

- Forty-six percent of all Indigenous people aged 15 to 64 years were not in the labor force in 2001 [compared to 27.0 percent of non-Indigenous people]. Only 4 percent were self-employed.

Income:

- Average income is A$226 per week for Indigenous people [A$380 per week for non-Indigenous people].
- This meant that people found it very difficult to raise A$2,000 in times of crisis (e.g. for hospitalization, a funeral, or car repairs).

Justice:

- In 1992 Indigenous people made up fourteen percent of the total prison population, which had increased by 2004 to twenty-one percent.

Family:

- 20.1 per 1,000 Indigenous children in 2001–2002 received out-of-home care; while for the non–Indigenous population it is 3.2 per 1,000.
- Substantiated child-abuse cases: In New South Wales, 15.3 per 1,000; [4.3 per 1,000]; Victoria 48.1 per 1,000 Indigenous cases [6.1 per 1,000 non-Indigenous cases]; and in the Northern

Territory 9.7 per 1,000 Indigenous cases [3.2 per 1,000 non-Indigenous cases].[36]

The present situation is marked by lack of a treaty, a faltering conversation about reconciliation (which many Indigenous people do not want anyway), and no formal national political voice. As the statistics show it is a reality of appalling social conditions. It is about continuing discrimination and racism. It is also about the struggle to make helpful advances in policy and practice inside old paradigms and relationships. Consider, for example, the recent apology to the stolen generation.

On Wednesday February 13, 2008, the Prime Minister made an historic apology to the Stolen Generations. His speech, and the actual apology were well thought out, compassionate, and inspiring. They built on apologies that had already been made by the churches.[37] It was a brave moment that has drawn forth praise from Indigenous people, and a sense that new things are possible.[38]

But it seems to me that we need to be wary of too early a celebration. Racist, exclusionary, and normative discourse is fairly old and well rehearsed in Australia, and is not easily removed with one apology. Take these signs:

- The prime minister has made it clear there will be no compensation, no genuine reparation for this terrible past.

- This grand gesture has not changed the intervention in the Northern Territory (which will be dealt with in some detail in chapter five).

- At that time the stance of the federal opposition leader on the apology had been ambiguous to say the least. He had previously indicated (December 2, 2007 and February 5, 2008) that he was unhappy with an apology, because these were things done by our

36. These statistics are from the Human Rights and Equal Opportunities Commission (HREOC), and were provided to me by Rev. Shayne Blackman, National Administrator, Uniting Aboriginal and Islander Christian Congress.

37. For example, in 1997 the Uniting Church made an apology to the people from the Stolen Generation who had passed through its institutions (Assembly minute 97.33.04).

38. See, for example, Mick Dodson (co-chairman of Reconciliation Australia and director of the National Centre for Indigenous Studies at the Australian National University), "Finally Their Voices Will Be Heard."

ancestors and not ourselves. Leading Liberal politician and past Health Minister Tony Abbott said "there was no general policy of removal but some part-Aboriginal children were taken into institutions against the wishes of their parents."[39] The denial of history continues.

- Social commentators like Keith Windschuttle continue to argue that the children were not stolen but taken for benign purposes, despite the research to the contrary.[40]

Commentators still speak of the need to move past these words to action that will "lift Indigenous people out of their plight," a view that still removes control from Indigenous people.

Conclusion

There are extraordinarily creative things being done by Indigenous people in order not just to survive but to live well in the face of the ongoing forces that seek to exclude them from life. There are healthy political organizations, emerging scholars, artists, dancers and film makers. People have established and sustained health services and legal aid services, fought against deaths in custody, demanded that the tale of stolen children be told, and continue to struggle over land.

As Mudrooroo says, Indigenous people and identity survive and are healthy because, whatever the enormous differences across the community and nation, they are bound by the importance of family and kinship. It is family and relationships, the kinship pattern that provides identity and unity. It is "where are you from, and who are your relatives," that provides identity and belonging. "This is the enduring structure of Us Mob which continues to survive, though it has consistently been under threat from the Master, who sought to destroy it and replace it with his type of family in which he was the ruler, the father, the protector, the station owner, the missionary, the police sergeant, the premier, the prime minister, the king."[41]

---

39. Abbott, "Yes, To Save a Legacy; Yes, to Heal the Generations."

40. Windschuttle, "Don't Let Facts Spoil the Day." See Parry, "Such a Longing" for a contrary, well-researched position.

41. Mudrooroo, *Us Mob*, 19–20.

If the church is to do theology in this country as Second peoples, it needs to deal with a history that still shapes the nation, and with the present reality—both good and bad. It needs to relate to, sit down with, and speak of faith alongside Indigenous people.

2

Fitting Invasion and Dis-Location into the European "World"

The Social Construction of Reality

HUMAN BEINGS FIND IT IMPOSSIBLE TO DEAL WITH THE THOUSANDS OF relationships and experiences that constitute their lives without relating them to a generalized framework or pattern of life that gives order and meaning to individual experiences. Any effort to relate to each individual person and situation as if it were a unique situation is too complex a task in anything more than a small village. Further, without patterns that explain and give sense to common elements in various social experiences, there is nothing to form the basis for shared existence.

Social existence is possible only as life is institutionalized—i.e., as various relationships are typified and are able to be more or less repeated in a variety of situations. Life is institutionalized when people are related to on the basis of particular roles, rather than on the basis of personal relationships. These roles carry more or less generally acceptable, and expected behavior patterns which make relationships predictable. For example, if a person hires a tradesperson or gets on a bus it is possible to expect certain behavior and knowledge regardless of what one knows of the particular tradesperson or bus driver. Because we are born into a particular world, with its language and symbols, it can seem that everything is "natural." It appears that such a "world" has an objective existence beyond the people who develop and support the way it is constructed. That is, what we know of the world seems to be what the world *is*. For example, gender roles can seem natural, or certain sexual roles can seem unnatural. In our day the centrality of the economy and economic growth can seem natural.

Yet the world as we know it is not a fixed, objective reality in which we all share. The patterns of relationships that exist in a community and, more important, the meaning given to the relationships, do not exist as an objective reality but emerge from the interaction between human action and reflection. We have been born into a world with a linguistic system, values, and definitions that precede us and that account for the way time and space are organized. This means that human lives and perceptions of meaning are structured by socially agreed and sanctioned modes of behavior. What seems real and normal to people in particular groups, classes, and communities is shaped by that particular group. The way the parts of the world are related, the value and priority that we give to various things, the way life is explained and justified, the goal or purpose of existence are socially constructed and expressed through the language and symbols that exist before us, into which we are born, and through which we negotiate our life. By "socially constructed" I mean that the world we live in is construed by the participants in a culture in terms of their particular knowledge, interests, power, and relationships; and people tacitly agree to behave as if this is the way the world actually is.[1]

There are probably any number of ways in which we could understand the central questions around which a community constructs its understanding of reality, but I find it helpful to think of three central questions:

- What is the good or flourishing life?

- How do we gain access to that life?

- What is stopping us getting that life, and how do we overcome that obstacle?

Implicit within these questions are also the questions:

- Who belongs to, and who is excluded from, the community or the good life?

---

1. Berger and Luckmann, *Social Construction of Reality*, were the first to use the term "social construction of reality." Other useful books are Hacking, *Social Construction of What?* and Searle, *Construction of Social Reality*.

- What right do I have to be in this place, on this land, within this good life?

- Is this all there is to human life, or is there something more?

- How do we know that our claims about the world are true or trustworthy?

This is not just the framework for a world shaped by a religious story. These are the questions that shape, for example, the narrative of consumer capitalism and its claims about what constitutes a good life, how that is earned or gained, the need for and possibility of constant growth and a better future, and on what basis one has a right to be part of it. As we shall see later in this chapter, it is also a framework that helps us understand the social construction of life and meaning in modern, invaded Australia.

Human thoughts and feelings are capable of being objectified in a way that makes them available to others. For example, lovers who are separated may objectify and convey their feelings by sending flowers or cards, the meaning of which is found in both the socially shared meaning of the symbols, and in their particular relationship. When a sign is intended to reveal not only the subjective feelings of another person but is intended to span spheres of reality (e.g., past and present, waking and dreaming), it can be defined as a symbol.[2] Symbols are used by a community to convey a sense of the meaning that lies behind immediate social reality. Symbols justify, explain, and support the social construction of reality. Most important for any society is the existence of those symbolic systems whose particular purpose is to explain the interrelationships that occur between institutions. These broad symbolic systems can be described as worldviews and can provide an overarching view of reality that attempts to explain the basis for the whole society.

Worldviews are often embodied in myths (i.e., a set of ideas that provides transcendent meaning, and that may or may not be religious). Myths give shape to the shared life of a community. These myths are spread throughout the community by the use of stories and by celebrations. The stories will usually be about creation, redemption, national and religious heroes, the nature of humankind, and the values and realities that constitute the meaning of the world. Each person has a

2. Berger and Luckmann, *Social Construction of Reality*, 55.

personal story that explains his or her myth, and a story, more or less like his or her own, that tells of the myths of society. Each group in society will pass to its members the particular experiences and memories of the community's history and activities, and its explanation of why the world is the way it is. This explanation will constitute a more-or-less set framework from within which people will judge the events that surround them. As Peter Berger points out, the myths that people hold remain in the background of their lives as unarticulated assumptions that are part of their character.[3] They are articulated, and actualized only in moments of social change and personal or social crisis. Even when the myths remain unspoken, they are still the basis on which people act.

While early social relationships are a major factor in shaping our perspectives, as we grow older we are confronted by a variety of understandings of the world, views that claim to offer the most meaningful perspective on the world. The relative claims of these worldviews cannot be judged on a logical basis, for they imply claims the truth of which can only be judged in the future. Thus all worldviews, be they religious or otherwise, involve faith choices. To a large extent, the faith choices that are made, the adoption of a particular social construction of reality, depend on what Juan Luis Segundo has called "*referential witnesses* in whom we believe."[4] That is, we adopt certain perspectives on the world because people we rely on indicate that they have found such a perspective to be meaningful in their journey through life.

The community sustains its view of the world and its life by retelling the stories that give it its distinctive life. From an early age people tell us stories: interesting, funny, fascinating, enjoyable, and scary stories. Mom and Dad tell us stories about Auntie Maude and her "friends," or about cousin Fred and his lack of regular work, or about the woman down the road who didn't have children because she was too busy working; and the tone and style of the stories tell us how the world should be. If we are part of a religious community, we hear stories through the liturgical and other practices of those communities. In our day we encounter important narratives though TV, movies, and other media.

The stories told to us by family, friends, and other people help us to understand what is to be valued; what we are to make of work, sport,

---

3. Berger, *Pyramids*, 32–33.
4. Segundo, *Faith and Ideologies*, 6 (italics original).

family, or marriage; how we are to deal with the difficult things in our life; who we should relate to; who are insiders and outsiders; what are the connections between things; what sense we can make of suffering and death; how we deal with evil; what the source is of human hope; and whether this is all there is to life, or whether there more. These stories help us build connection with others, allow us to see where we fit in the web of relationships that surround us, and teach us our place in the world. Each of these things helps us build our own story about life and find our own sense of what life is supposed to mean. The primary sense of our life will be our own experience and observation, but experience means more than being there—wherever "there" is. Experience is about figuring out what is going on, and for that we need the accumulated moral wisdom of our community.

There is an ideological dimension to the way a community describes social reality in the sense of "ideas serving as weapons for social interests."[5] This is not to deny that there are facts, either social or historical. It is to claim that the way these facts are integrated into a person's world depends on a previous, socially constructed understanding of reality. That the First Fleet sailed to Australia in 1787–1788 is a fact. Why that occurred, and what meaning it has for the present reality is a judgment dependent on a particular view of reality.

The issue of ideology is important for theology, both because it is closely tied to the issue of social construction of reality, and because religion is often dismissed as an oppressive ideology. I believe that religious faith and theology are ideological in the sense that they contribute to the production of ideas and meaning. They are also ideological in the Marxist sense—that theological ideas are social products: they arise in particular social communities and relationships, and they reflect the agenda and interests of those who do theology. This is not to say that ideas have no force or are simply a reflection of materialist concerns. The relationship between ideas and social forces is much more complex and dialogical than that. The important thing is for the theologian to learn "to be attentive to the *limits* imposed on their discourse and imagination by their historical and social location."[6] One role of theology as

5. Berger and Luckmann, *Social Construction of Reality*, 18.

6. Lash, *Theology on the Way to Emmaus*, 131 (italics original). The whole of chapter 8, "Theory, Theology and Ideology" is quite helpful in regard to ideology and knowledge.

a consciously self-reflective exercise is to question those expressions of faith that are unaware of their social foundations (and their pattern of social division and dominance), of the interests that they represent, and their claim to false universality.

The difficulty with the classical understanding of social construction of reality and ideology was that it assumed a too-homogenous view of culture and a too-simple view of the nature of reality. It seemed to assume that culture was largely a universal, all-encompassing reality in which only a few people (or a class) had effective control and shaped the way the world was understood. It assumed a world constructed almost exclusively by elites. Recent cultural analysis and criticism provides a more complex understanding of culture, which is important to the way we understand the role of theology. Such analysis speaks of culture as pluralistic, conflictual, and without a unifying core that can guarantee stable identities. The heart of this cultural dynamic "is the struggle for and the negotiation of power."[7] This world is always a contested world— both in terms of the way life is organized (relationships and power) and the narratives and symbols that explain that world. In many cases the ideologies that reinforce the world are hidden, and we act without any conscious awareness. In some theories this has been called hegemony and is concerned for the way in which elites control knowledge and power.

I think that the world is much more contested than hegemony suggests, and that there are many strands and narratives within any one community that work against absolute control and uniformity. There is no pure culture that is distinct from every other culture, and no self-contained social group. Each culture is cobbled out of a multitude of actions, discourse, and social practice, and is constantly emerging, transient, and contested. In other words, all cultures are hybrid, the distinctiveness of a culture emerging in its (temporary) new way of bringing the pieces together.[8] "Or, as Betsy Taylor puts it, culture is an emergent performance, a temporary production of a shared way to go that is always shifting and emerging from a bodied, interactive negotiation."[9]

7. Davaney, "Theology and the Turn to Cultural Analysis," in Brown et al., *Converging on Culture*, 6.

8. Fulkerson, "We Don't See Color Here," in Brown et al., *Converging on Culture*, 61–96.

9. Ibid., 147. This came from a conversation between Taylor and Fulkerson.

In this understanding of culture, ordinary people do not passively accept or consume culture, but contribute to the shape of culture at many levels, including through localized practices, identities, and meaning narratives. They are also not simply the object of power, for power is more diffuse and is constantly being reconfigured and renegotiated. It is also true that people do not live inside a world of ideas but of relationship and practices shaped by story and ritual. They build a way of living based on a network of important relationships, patterns of living, the ability to exercise control over their own lives, and stories that make sense of and integrate this in some way. That is, ideas emerge from particular social contexts and relationships.

The importance of this discussion of the social construction of reality is to remind us that what we take as normal and "just there" is actually formed in the contested world of social relationships and power. What we accept as normal is only normal for some people, yet we often assume *our* normalcy as unquestionably universal. Others are expected to measure their life against ours. The world as we understand it—the world of racism, power, justice, relationships, and economy—is shaped by our social location and by the interests that we seek to protect as Christians and the church. We each know the world from our own perspective. It is not possible to have any knowledge at all without prejudice, perspective, or viewpoint.

Constructing a World around Invasion

Colonial expansion assumes that such expansion will contribute to the good life within the imperial community, at least among some members. The question always is whether anyone within the colonized land will also have access to that life, however it is defined. In Australia, invasion, dispossession, and continuing occupation make the claim that the new life to be established within this place is not open to the original inhabitants. The violence, dispossession from land, imprisonment, segregation, stolen children, and continuing marginalization are statements that Indigenous people are to remain apart, outside, and invisible.

The narrative worldview that is constructed around those events and claims seeks to answer some of the issues raised above:

- What are the signs that people are able to be part of this good life? That is, are they civilized and Christian enough, are they human enough, to be part of the new society?

- What rights do the Indigenous people have to the land, to a place in this new society?

- How do we know that these claims are true? In Australia this is a question that suggests a clash between the emerging scientific worldview and the Christian worldview.

The answers to these questions, woven into a complex worldview, is that Indigenous people were not fully human (a claim supported by the rising scientific racism), they were not civilized enough to participate in this new society, that they had no rights to the land, and that they gave up the land without a struggle. It is a narrative explanation that denies Indigenous claims and experience and further makes them invisible. History is normalized within a dominant worldview. It is a world shaped by the myth of *terra nullius*, various expressions of racism, and the denial of history. Theologically it implicitly makes the claim that the God of Christian faith is not located among us in a way that matters for Indigenous people.

Terra Nullius and Not People

Those who entered Australia assumed that Indigenous people around the world were not civilized enough to exercise the kind of sovereignty over their land that would enable them to participate in international politics. So the European powers assumed sovereignty and set up colonies. While such claims to sovereignty did not automatically abrogate native people's title to land, in Australia this is exactly what was claimed. Those who entered Australia had no interest in negotiation or purchase of land. As far as they were concerned, it was a wide open country whose land was there for the taking—to be farmed, settled, and sold for as much profit as possible. And when it was objected that they should not take land in this way, they fell back on the legal fiction of *terra nullius*.

Terra nullius literally means "empty and unoccupied." It does not mean that there were not people, but that those people had no claim to ownership of the land. The issue of ownership of land rested on the assumption of European law that ownership was based on agriculture and permanent occupation. The evidences of occupancy were reckoned to be boundary markers or fences to separate properties, houses to mark permanent occupation, and tilled soil to mark the addition of labor. These factors were though to be missing in Australia, and so it was assumed that Aboriginal people had no legal or moral claim to the land. This legal fiction of *terra nullius*, finally overturned by the High Court in *the Eddie Mabo v. Murray Island* decision of 1992, was spelled out in the Northern Territory Supreme Court by Justice Richard Blackburn, in the case of *Milirrpum v. Nabalco* (1971). He says: "(b) 'there is a distinction between settled colonies, where the land, being desert and uncultivated, is claimed by right of occupancy, and conquered or ceded colonies . . .' (c) 'the colony of New South Wales belonged to the class of settled colonies; that is to say, that it was a colony which consisted of a tract of territory practically unoccupied without settled inhabitants or settled law, at the time when it was peacefully annexed to the British dominions.'"[10] That is, while Blackburn acknowledged a clear relationship between Indigenous people and land, he ruled that their interest was not comparable with English common law precedents in regard to property interests, that they had no title to land under European law, and that any rights they might have had were terminated by the relevant Northern Territory Mining ordinance. Blackburn, of course, was simply quoting the Privy Council, which in 1889 had declared that Australia "consisted of a tract of territory practically unoccupied" (*Cooper v. Stuart* (1889) 14 AC at p. 291).[11]

The difficulty we have in understanding the argument about nonownership is that the modern debate has been shaped by a partial understanding of Indigenous society and by relatively recent legal arguments about *terra nullius*. Indigenous society was complex and varied greatly across Australia. In the southern areas the people were settled, lived in houses, and harvested and cultivated the land and the sea. Those who moved into areas like Victoria knew that the people were settled and owned the land, but they swept across the land and destroyed the people because they had the power to do so. Their justification was

---

10. *Milpirrum v. Nabalco Pty Ltd* (1971), 17 FLR 141. Henry Reynolds has provided a more detailed account of *terra nullius* in *The Law of the Land*, and "Frontier History after Mabo," 4–11.

11. Quoted in Brennan, "Aboriginal Aspirations to Land: Unfinished History and a Continuing National Responsibility," in Brennan et al., *Finding Common Ground*, 13.

racist—that these were no real people. Villages were destroyed, and signs of occupancy were obliterated. Those who followed, a generation or two later, and who sought to construct a mythology of brave explorers and settlers going where no one had gone before, could safely do so because a culture had been destroyed. The land had been empty when their ancestors arrived, or so the story could be told.

In the more northern areas the people did lead a more nomadic life and had fewer of the markers that Europeans would recognize as signs of land ownership. There it was easier to pretend that the land was empty and unoccupied. It is no accident that it was in regard to land claims in that area that Justice Blackburn made his ruling.

The point, though, is that there was often no need for justification, and no calling to account. Indigenous people had no rights and no voice, and few others had the courage to stand up and speak on their behalf. It was only when Indigenous people in Arnhem Land, with the support of the Methodist Church, found their voice and claimed their land in the face of the encroachment of mining companies that justification for past actions became necessary. At this point the old doctrine of *terra nullius* was reclaimed to deny people their life and their rights.

Even if *terra nullius* has been overturned as a legal doctrine, there is still a strong sense in Australian culture that we only own land when we buy it and use it productively. The way into the good life is not traditional and ancient ownership of land but the ability and willingness to participate in the economy. There is a belief that sacred sites are invented as a way of claiming land. There is little acknowledgement that Indigenous people still claim that they own the land and have never given it away or stopped claiming that it is theirs. The issue for them is not about reclaiming land but about having their ownership recognized.

Racism

The question that is faced by colonists and invaders is, are these a people that needed to be treated with the same rights and respect that we give to our own people? That is, can we justify our actions in regard to these people because they are not really equal people?

Prejudice is my personal feelings about another and may arise from my fear of strangers or of those who are different. Prejudice is about the other being "other" and often ends as the other is assimilated and becomes like me. Racism, on the other hand, has to do with the belief that a particular group of people are inferior by reason of an unchangeable biological nature. Racism is more than my feelings; it has a social function. Racism explains and justifies the place that another group has in society and, most often, why they are oppressed, enslaved, excluded, and marginalized. Racism has to do with the social location of people's body in time and space in relation to the body politic, with the social power to enforce racist structures and social location, and with the stories and symbols that explain and justify that world. Racism assumes that different people can be ranked hierarchically according to their worth, and that differences do not depend on history and social communities but blood.[12]

Racism justifies or "explains" the inferior place of people in society in many ways: the people are morally inferior or dangerous, they are incapable of learning, they are childlike and needing to be looked after (e.g., they cannot be trusted to make their own decisions or to use money in a responsible manner), they are at the bottom of the "great chain of being"[13] and are to be treated as curiosities like kangaroos or platypuses, or they are dirty and uncivilized. Racism has an ideological purpose and role in the social construction of reality and in the justification of the harm done to another.

Modern racism arose in the pursuit of national identity and the defining of the nation-state (the need to provide a sense of national identity), and in the need to justify colonial expansion. It sought to respond to the question that was raised by the discovery of new lands and new people: where do these new people fit into the purposes of God? Within the Christian cosmology contact with the new "other" that occurred with colonial expansion posed the question, are you savable within the Christian understanding of the world? That is, contact with the "other" poses the question of whether this "other" is human, is one

12. Anne Pattel-Gray has a helpful discussion of race, stereotypes, prejudice, and racism (including white racism) in *Great White Flood*, chap. 1.

13. Baldwin Spenser in *Guide to the Australian Ethnographical Collection in the National Museum of Victoria* (Melbourne: Public Library, Museums and National Gallery, 1901) said that Tasmanians were "living representatives of palaeolithic man, lower in the scale of culture than any human beings now upon earth" (8); quoted in Pattel-Gray, *Great White Flood*, 87.

created in the image of God, and is descendent from the common parents Adam and Eve.

This debate about the humanness of indigenous people had been around since Europeans began their expansion. As early as 1550 Charles V of Spain called for a debate about whether the Indians of the Caribbean were human beings of equal worth to Europeans in the sight of God. Clearly this debate was not simply about where people fitted into Christian anthropology, but about whether or not it was okay to kill them and drive them from their land The result was a debate between two priests: Batolomé de Las Casas and Juan Gines de Sepulveda. Casas had witnessed the Spanish conquest of the Caribbean first hand and was appalled by what he saw. He was convinced from the Scriptures and from experience that these Indians were real people for whom Jesus had died. Sepulveda saw the issue as a philosopher schooled in Aristotle and Aquinas, and sought to demonstrate that the Indians were lesser humans, the barbarians of that world. Only force or death could make them subservient to the state and the church. Casas won the debate, but in reality the slaughter continued, as did the debate about the will of God for peoples in invaded lands.

In Australia, Christian control of cosmology and worldview was under question by the new world of reason and scientific knowledge. A part of the justification for racism and colonial expansion was found in the sciences and their pseudoscientific offshoots. The issues of self-differentiation and commonality were caught up in the growing concern for classification, which lead to phrenology (skull reading) and other practices and theories. The question in that intellectual world or framework, quite different from the Christian world, was, "Are you orderable within the scientific taxonomy of a civilized European humanity?' The quest for conversion, here, is replaced, not simply by a drive to civilize, but also subtly, by an impulse to classify"[14] For example, in 1858 Thomas McCrombie proposed to the Victorian Legislative Council of which he was a member that that there be an enquiry into the condition of Aboriginal people and how to help them. A Committee of Enquiry was appointed. There was much debate in the Committee about the place of Indigenous people in the plan of God, but it is the frontispiece of the 1859 report of the Committee that is most telling. It is a drawing of two Indigenous men

14. Perkinson, *White Theology*, 68.

and twelve skulls. Phrenology was seen as a science, and the committee believed that skulls could show the line between one group of humans and another. "At least, that was what some hoped for from phrenology: an alternative map of human difference in which the distinctive cranial features of each race revealed the physical reality of divergent ability, and gave lie to the concept of 'One Blood.'"[15] In other words, this was pseudo-scientific support for the view that Indigenous people were not really human in the way Europeans were; they were a different species. This discipline provided support for the view that human beings were actually part of the great chain of being, but that Indigenous people were further down the scale, and in the world of evolution would simply have to give way before a superior people. This was justified either as a providential act of God or as the survival of the fittest.

Stephen Mueke says that in Australia relationships and discourse with Indigenous people is shaped by racism, romanticism (which reflects the attraction of the so-called primitive and uncivilized), and anthropological discourse.[16] Racism is constructed through the use of metaphors and the way grammar operates within community discourse. Racist discourse does two things. "It utilizes a series of metaphors that displace the designation of people away from adult humans to children, animals and inanimate objects, which are subject only to the laws of nature. The other feature is that of essentialism, or geneticism. This structures discourse in such a way that social conditions, or whatever is going on, are seen as the effect of people's genes, their essential racial difference."[17] In Muecke's form of discourse, "romanticism" has to do with the view that these "poor people" are going to die out. It justifies involvement (interference?) in people's lives on the basis of compassion and care. Anthropological discourse speaks in ways that make its claims count as knowledge, as fact. Anthropological discourse "maintains the power to articulate the terms in which differences can be stated."[18]

The most insidious and most widespread form of racism is paternalism. This form of racism sees Indigenous people as passive victims, as people who do not actively participate in history, as people that one

15. Kenny, *The Lamb Enters the Dreaming*, 50–51. See chapter 4, "Noah's Curse," for a fuller discussion of the debate about Indigenous humanity.

16. Muecke, *Textual Spaces*, 24–35.

17. Ibid., 32.

18. Ibid., 27.

must feel sorry for, and that one must do things for. It is a racism that subtly degrades Aboriginal culture and ignores or denies the complexity of Aboriginal culture or of the warriors who defended the land from European invasion. It is a racism that assumes that Aboriginal culture is of very little value, that traditional society was very primitive, and that Aboriginal people need to adopt the values and lifestyle of mainstream European society. It is one that cannot imagine the construction of a national heritage that draws on both fifty thousand years of history and the cultural heritage of the Second people.

Racism in Australia was based on the need for cheap labor and on a hierarchical social order that did not consider people equal (and thus the unequals could be enslaved without any real justification). Mark Francis suggests that racism in Australia (at least in the period he is dealing with: 1880–1920) was constructed on the basis of government control and was "often designed to inhibit any social change which originated outside official circles."[19] Now that it was acknowledged that Indigenous people and society would survive, they had to be controlled. Evidence for this controlling behavior is found in a large number of books written by both Indigenous authors and whites, some of which are cited in the bibliography. Sally Dingo's account of the Dingo family in Western Australia highlights the control exercised over Aboriginal lives by every white person they encountered—police, station managers, Protectors, government officials, clergy, and ordinary people. She tells of the appalling living conditions, of the segregated living on the edges of towns, of living in tin humpies without electricity or water, of the need to prove that you were a "better class of Aboriginal person" to be allowed to marry or receive a pension. There was the constant fear that children could be taken away, and the poverty that comes from years of work with no pay.[20]

Racism in Australia was at times filled with a deep savagery. Men were subjected to savage beatings and sexual mutilation, and women to violent sex and abuse. Whips were used without thought against women and men, boys and girls. I think this violence is a response to a sense of attraction and sexual desire for what is seen as the wonderfully wild, the uncivilized, and the natural in Indigenous people. There is a fear that

19. Francis, "Social Darwinism," 96.
20. Dingo, *The Story of Our Mob.*

this desire will engulf one, will draw one into a loss of civilization, of humanity, or salvation, and will foster a sense of shame. This fear leads to violence and anger, to the effort to destroy that which threatens one's life, wholeness, and salvation. In a very real sense, this is the outworking of the romantic idea of the noble savage (i.e., both noble and savage). Any effort to deal with racism in Australian society must not just deal in some calm way with prejudice or with injustice, but with this emotional dimension of racism.

The most difficult and far-reaching point of racism, that which confronts Second peoples, and is hardest to see or shake off, is the assumption—the unowned, unaware assumption—of the normalcy of what is "white." Whiteness is seen as wholeness, as in some sense soteriological. Or, as James Perkinson says, "White identity is generally lived, that is to say, as a kind of 'artless ignorance,' an almost incorrigible lack of awareness of either one's racial position or the actual cost to others of one's prosperity."[21] It distorts what starts out as well-intentioned action into racist oppression. For example, in order to protest rape and violence against women, the World Council of Churches initiated a campaign called Thursdays in Black. Women were asked to wear black as a protest against rape, violence, and death. Yet what did such a campaign mean for black women? Their color was used as a sign of mourning and was linked to rape and destruction. It was an insensitive and racist campaign, promoted without consultation with a community where such abuse was rife.[22]

Another example of the impact of assumptions about the normalcy of whiteness is the 1967 referendum to allow Indigenous people to be counted in the census, to be placed on the electoral rolls as citizens, and to have laws made by the federal government. This is celebrated as a great event and as a wonderful advance, and in some ways it was. But why do we celebrate the granting of rights by referendum to a people who, like the rest of the nation, should have had these rights by birth? A right which people claim they are able to confer on another is also a right that can be withdrawn. The right of Indigenous people to be citizens is conferred not as a right but as a privilege controlled by others.

---

21. Perkinson, *White Theology*, 89.
22. Pattel-Gray, *Great White Flood*, 183.

We again claim to be normal and demand the right to determine when others are also acceptable within that norm.

A significant feature of racism in Australia was a view of the superiority of British civilization. From the very beginning there was an assumption that Indigenous people would need to be civilized. Part of the assumption about the superiority of British civilization was the claim that colonial expansion was good for the world because of British benevolence. There was a view that people and nations were actually fortunate that they had been invaded (politically and economically) by the British Empire. The empire was seen as a force for good, one that delivered economic benefits and democracy.

In an extraordinarily disturbing book on the relationship between British imperial policy and famine, Mike Davis makes the well-documented claim that racial and colonial arrogance, inflexible free-market ideology, the desire to support the British industrial complex and colonial war efforts, and an almost total disregard for life led to famines that killed between 12.2 and 29.3 million Indian people between 1876 and 1902.[23] The British government, with the support of industry, actively discouraged the development of skilled workers, denied contracts to Indian firms who produced goods that could be imported from England, undermined the local textile industry, and generally discouraged an Indian-based industrial structure. India was, subsequently, the major importer of British consumer products. Yet, despite the so-called benevolence of British rule, income fell, life expectancy fell, and death levels were horrendous. "If the history of British rule in India were to be condensed into a single fact, it is this: there was no increase in India's per capita income from 1757 to 1947 ... Moreover in the age of Kipling, that 'glorious imperial half century' from 1872 to 1921, the life expectancy of ordinary Indians fell by a staggering 20 percent, a deterioration in human health probably without precedent in the subcontinent's long history of war and invasion."[24] The people of India were ruthlessly incorporated into the British trade and economy, with the consequence that their industry was discouraged, their food was exported, and their social structure was undermined as their economy was destroyed, and traditional mutual obligations became impossible.

23. Davis, *Late Victorian Holocausts*, 7.
24. Ibid., 311–12.

Australia was similarly incorporated into that economy and even into the military activities and campaigns (like the Boer War). Indigenous people were not drawn into this but were, rather, swept aside in order for their land to be used for the production of wool and other products. The claim that they would die out was not a plaintive cry but, one suspects, both a hope and a belief based on the claim that all so-called inferior races would pass away before the superior people of Europe.

Land Rights, Mabo, and Postmodern Racism

On January 26, 1976, the federal government, under the leadership of the then–prime minister, Malcolm Fraser, established the Northern Territory Land Rights Act. This Act gave Indigenous people the ability to claim unoccupied crown land and control of existing reserves, and provided them with the ability to control mining. The Act also established Land Councils and gave people the ability to make their voices heard by white Australia. This led to the cry that Indigenous people controlled too much land and had too much power.[25]

In June 1992, in response to a claim by Eddie Mabo, and others of sovereignty over the Murray Islands (off Queensland's coast), the High Court provided a ruling that overturned the myth of *terra nullius* and significantly changed the political landscape in Australia. The Mabo decisions recognized a system of land tenure prior to British occupation and allowed that such tenure could still exist under certain circumstances (including shared control of pastoral leases). The Labor government passed the Native Title Act (1993) and opened up further claims to be heard and dealt with. This, too, drew a backlash from the white community, and powerful interests took the matter to the High Court, where the Wik decision (1996) found that two forms of title could coexist. This finding was rendered inoperable when the by-then Liberal government passed the Native Title Act (1998).

Ken Gelder and Jane Jacobssuggest that the form of racism has changed.[26] They make a distinction between a colonial romantic and a postcolonial postmodern racism. In the earlier form of racism, there

---

25. There have been various attempts to change the land rights legislation, and to alter sacred sites legislation. See Broome, *Aboriginal Australians*, chap. 12.

26. Gelder and Jacobs, *Uncanny Australia*.

was little engagement between the two communities and an assumption that Indigenous people would be civilized (and probably converted to Christianity) and might even die out. Today's racism grows out of the meeting of Indigenous "sacred" and mainstream Australian society because of the recognition of land rights and sacred sites. This is a racism that comes from the confrontation caused by legal recognition of rights and by the challenge to privilege. It is a racism that claims that Indigenous people now have "too much." Naming this as "postcolonial racism" the authors say, "This is a form of racism (and we need not use these inverted commas any more) which sees Aboriginal people as lacking on the one hand—in which case, one will feel sympathy, guilt, shame, etc.—and having 'too much' on the other, in which case one feels 'resentment.' The problem in contemporary Australia is: *at what point does the one become the other?*"[27]

Racism in this form is again about control of access to power, resources, and place, and is a response to the challenge to the rights that white people assume and take for granted. It is a racism that arises in response to the claim that rights actually exist within Indigenous communities, to the affirmation of Indigenous people's humanity that is inherent in the Mabo decisions, and to the view of what is normal in Second people's society. The Mabo decisions allow Indigenous people to make claims within a competitive framework around land use that now denies mining companies and pastoralists the right to make all decisions. It has produced a complaint from those with enormous power that they are now embattled minorities who need the protection of the government (a great inversion of the story of power).

We see this racism most clearly in the contest over mining and the protection of sacred space. It is a racism that again seeks to define Indigenous people and their religious life in ways that allow for their lives to be ignored or controlled. For example, in his book *Jabiluka*, Tony Grey, the founder of Pancontinental Mining, seeks to redefine Indigenous religious life in order to allow for escape from the negotiations required by the Aboriginal Land Rights Act. He suggests that Land Councils are not really Aboriginal bodies but bureaucracies open to manipulation by the interest of others. He argues that land is a deeply

---

27. Gelder and Jacobs, *Uncanny Australia*, 17 (italics original).

spiritual thing, but that there is no real sense of ownership or possession as that is understood in European society.[28]

But modern racism, like racism of old, is not simply big-picture disagreements and arguments about power and voice in issues of land and sacred sites. It is about daily living and ordinary relationships. Being a white person means that I live with privileges and rights of access that I take for granted, and that I see as a normal part of life. "White Australians never have considered that because of their white skin, they have gained all manner of privileges—such as the ease with which they can cash a cheque, or walk through a department store without being under suspicion by the store detectives, or know that their colour can never be used against them when applying for jobs, or renting houses, or when relating to police, or to public authorities, or even to hairdressers when in a salon."[29]

Even in the church this can be so. White people do not see their own color, or how their life and position is simply accepted as normal. They do not see how easy it is for them to speak, make decisions, or exercise power in a gathering with Indigenous people (or even in a more multicultural gathering). The position and tradition of the white church is seen as normal, and other people must earn their place and work to have their voice heard. There is never an equal conversation, because the starting point and implicit understanding of what is the status quo is already set by color. There is a need for greater awareness of how this world of color shapes relationships and power.

Invisibility

Racism, I would suggest, is primarily about social location .The struggle of racist societies is to ensure that people "know their place." In Australia, Indigenous people were constantly taught "their place" by exclusion from schools, work, and proper housing; by their separation in cinemas and pubs; by their place in the criminal justice system and relationships with police; by racist taunts and the treatment and stereotyping they receive in the media and in school textbooks; and by the violence that they sustained. Racism in Australia involves a history of destruction, and removing Indigenous people from places that are too close to white

28. Grey, *Jabiluka*.
29. Pattel-Gray, *Great White Flood*, 209.

society, ignoring people, segregating them, and assimilating them so that they no longer exist as a separate group.

My central claim is that the primary shape of racism in Australia in regard to Indigenous people is one of invisibility and one of making visible for the purposes of shame. Shame arises not, as in the New Testament, around rules about purity or, as in the Middle Ages, around mores about relationships. It arises as shame about having no place in the framework of a consumerist economy that defines people as consumers and by what they own and possess. This invisibility shows in denying Indigenous people citizenship, in taking their children, in imprisoning them, in denying them the vote, and in taking land. The point is that if people are kept invisible and silent, if history can be denied, there is no challenging event to reshape the character of the nation.

The Denial of History

The movement of Indigenous people towards self-determination has carried with it a claim that history needs to be acknowledged. It is a claim that their place in this society has been shaped by the nature of contact between the two communities. It carries a desire for apology, for recognition, for the honoring of their experience and not its denial.

But there continues to be a denial of history at three levels:

- There was no destruction of Indigenous people, no massacres, and no frontier wars. We see this most recently in the history wars.

- Even if these things happened, you cannot blame us because we didn't do it, shouldn't have to apologize for what others did, and cannot be held responsible to ensure that some reparation takes place.

- People shouldn't go on about the past. They should simply forgive and move forward.

There Were No Massacres and No Destruction

In the face of claims to self-determination by Indigenous people, which have led to a reclaiming of history, there have been recent efforts to rewrite history on the basis that the so-called "Black Armband" view of history is simply incorrect. The emphasis has been on peaceful settlement, on the benign treatment of children taken from their parents, on a denial of massacres, and on a need for national unity. This view is reflected in the then–Prime Minister John Howard's speech in the Commonwealth parliament in October 1996: "I profoundly reject . . . the black armband view of Australian history. I believe the balance sheet of Australian history is overwhelmingly a very generous and benign one . . . we have a remarkably positive history."[30] What the former prime minister meant was that recent history writing was too negative and gave too much space to past wrongs. Indeed the assertion is made that the occupation of Australia was relatively peaceful.

This conversation about history, which has been going on in the media for some years, found its lightening rod among historians with the publication of Keith Windschuttle's *The Fabrication of History*.[31] Windschuttle challenged the trustworthiness of the oral history of Indigenous people and denied the extent of the massacres in Tasmania. There have been significant responses from a number of scholars.[32] The debate is, most significantly, about what will be recognized as our history, what will shape our common life and identity, and who we see ourselves to be. As Bruce Pascoe says: "How do we as a nation resolve to express our history? By scrubbing out whole unpalatable events, averting our face from the dispossessed, pretending they are unworthy of God's love? Or do we aim to become a *civilised* society attempting to encompass the entire history of existence."[33]

History is not simply the act of collating facts that exist for the finding by the scholar. Historians select events, and arrange them into a coherent pattern that coheres to the assumptions they start with. As Stuart Macintyre and Anna Clark suggest, "The facts do not exist prior to the interpretation that establishes their significance. Rather, historical research involves a continuous dialogue between the two."[34] The interpretation of history occurs from within worldviews and acts

30. Howard, Speech to the House of Representatives, 30 October 1996 (*Parliamentary Debates*, House Official Hansard, Wednesday, 30 October 1996), 1658.

31. Windschuttle, *The Fabrication of History*.

32. Manne, *Whitewash*; Macintyre and Clark, *The History Wars*. Brett Furner has provided quite a helpful summary of the issues and some of the people involved in "An/Other Australian Theology," in Pearson, *Faith in a Hyphen*, 232–35, n. 57.

33. Pascoe, *Convincing Ground*, 220.

34. Macintyre and Clark, *The History Wars*, 29.

to challenge or reinforce the social construction of reality. Arguments over history are struggles over the ability to control the past, and over the place it will play in the present. History is about identity, and how we think about ourselves. It is about present relationships, and how the past plays out in those relationships. In this case it is about the validity of oral history, and the insistence of scholars like Windschuttle that only their historical methods have any validity and provide genuine evidence, and that people of an oral tradition have no voice. It is about whether Indigenous people actually suffered in the past, and who has a right to speak with authority about that experience of suffering.

We Didn't Do It

Along with opposing a so-called black-armband view of history, John Howard also held to the view that we are not responsible for the past, we didn't harm Indigenous people, and we shouldn't apologize for what others did in another time. The prime minister made this very clear when the *Bringing Them Home* report was tabled in Parliament on May 26, 1997.

The position that we are not responsible for the actions of another generations flows easily from a very individualistic understanding of human life and from the view that we all make our own lives regardless of history or culture. It allows people to claim responsibility for lives that owe a great deal to birth, family, inheritance, and social location. It allows people to avoid responsibility for the way in which history still impacts on the present. We live in a wealthy country that was built on dispossession. We claim ownership of land that is and was Indigenous land.

Forget the Past and Move On

When the issue of an apology is raised, as it was with the Stolen Generations, there are always those who say we should just forget about what happened and move on. There is nothing we can do about the past, so let's live in the present. For example, Geoff Wraight reports that in a research project carried out towards the end of the 1990s, 80 percent of people said that "Everyone should stop talking about the way Aboriginal people were treated in the past, and just get on with the future."[35]

John Hirst offers an interesting slant on that debate when he says that all the arguments in the history wars about how many were killed are irrelevant. He says that those who argue that numbers matter are really suggesting that conquest could have happened more peacefully and in a better manner—a claim that he disputes through an illustration from the treatment of Native Americans. He says that in reality the whole place belonged to Indigenous people, and that it was conquered. Conquest is always difficult and bloody and hurtful, and it is not possible to imagine world history without conquest.[36]

The difficulty with his position is that it suggests that the *nature* of our past relationship is irrelevant to our present, and that nothing of our character is shown by how we have acted in the past and by the way we claim and explain that action. If I hurt you once, it may speak of an aberration or an accident; but if I harm you continually, then it speaks of my character and raises other questions about our relationship. And if I harm you, I need to act in ways that acknowledge my action, if only as a way of saying that your sense of life and experience is true. My apology affirms your experience and does not further deny it. My apology suggests that I want to build a different relationship, and I would suggest, that I wish to take actions that might change what history has done.

Conclusion: The Way Forward

The present is filled with courage and struggle. Most significantly it is a time of new frontiers, as Indigenous people reject the old centers and claims of victory, and assert that some battles are continuing. Land rights remains on the agenda, joined by treaty and a preamble for the national constitution. Racism is being named in new forms, and people are fighting against abuse, unemployment, lack of education, poor health, and inadequate housing. The church is again being asked to consider where it sits at the frontier—that place where life is contested and claims have not been settled—and where it expects to encounter God. Its answer will depend in part on how it deals with and finds a new place in

35. Wraight, *Contours of an Australian Christology*, 74.
36. Hirst, *Sense & Nonsense*, 86.

relation to the world that has been constructed over the last 220 years to explain and justify the relationships that have existed in this land.

There are five central marks of this context for the task of theology:

1. The way racism is still part of our life, and the way it shapes our perceptions and discourse and relatedness.

2. The fact that we as Second peoples and as church live on stolen land.

3. The fact that our relationships in this land were based on violence, a violence that still distorts those relationships.

4. The social location of the church, and the way this effects both the way the church sees, and the interests it continues to protect.

5. The continuing marginalization of Indigenous people in most areas of life.

The challenge in this context is an awareness of how easily we see our race, our social location, our understanding of the church as normal, and how unconscious this assumption of normalcy is. It is the challenge of seeing how easily we move to normalize any challenges to our place and theology, and how our seeming openness to Indigenous people can cover a desire to control outcomes and to determine the conditions of the conversation. It is the challenge to our social location in the centre of power, in the theological tradition of white, male, European scholars. It is the challenge to the belief that we can describe our faith and church within our present social location and apart from our relationship with Indigenous people. For the church there is the challenge of building a relationship with a community whose sociality and common identity has its foundation in earth and in relationships; that is, in another religious tradition. It is to be challenged to revisit the relationship between cultural identity and religious life, both in terms of our temptation to make Christianity European, and in terms of the need to deal with the place of traditional spirituality in the life of Indigenous Christian people.

3

Theology as the Art of Naming Where God Is

Introduction

THEOLOGY IS THE CHURCH'S CONVERSATION ABOUT GOD, AND HOW
God touches and relates to the world. It plays a role in constructing and
supporting particular worlds, and theologians do their work from within particular social locations. Theology is about power—the power to
represent and construct the world. Theologians always protects certain
(often unconscious) interests—one's place in the world, who one listens
to and privileges in the conversation, and what set of values and beliefs
one "naturally" sits in and has made part of one's life. Theology arises
from people who have a particular social location in which power and
privilege and different social networks as well as race, gender, knowledge, class, and wealth are important.

All theology is necessarily contextual. Human beings are finite
creatures, not only in the sense that they die, but also in that they live
within the limits of a particular tradition that is bound by time and
place[1] (and, thus, by particular language and discourse, knowledge and
views of the world). When theology claims to be about universals, it
is claiming that particular interests should be accepted by everyone.
Particular contextual theologies arise to challenge the way theology is
controlled, and the way "normal" is determined. Those who claim to
hold universal truths are seeking to cover sectional interests by claiming to be beyond any such interest.

---

1. Hall says that this place is not simply location "but also state and condition, as in
the phrase 'knowing one's place' or 'the place of something or someone'" (*The Cross in
Our Context*, 44). It is both a geographic area and a shared human condition.

Contextual theology challenges the view that theology is simply reflection on Scripture and tradition seen as two unchanging and culturally neutral resources, and insists that present human experience is a crucial part of the theological task. It wrestles with the sources of theology and with the weight given to them and with how trustworthy the sources are when compiled by one section of society (e.g., white men). Contextual theologies are not content to simply accept the way the tradition is usually read and to see what it means in particular contexts. It also seeks to reread the tradition, to ask what interests are reflected in that tradition and who is excluded, and to ask questions of the tradition from within the particular context.

In this chapter I want to suggest what the theological task might look like in Australia for Second peoples if we take account of the context—historical and social—and of our own social location and interests. I am concerned about what we are doing when we do theology.[2] Of course I am far from being the first to attempt to construct an Australian theology. Beginning with a series of essays edited by Victor Hayes,[3] there have been a number of major works, including recent studies about cross-cultural theology in Australia.[4] While acknowledging their important and pioneering work, it is not my intention to consciously engage with them but, rather, to set out on the task of a theology for Second peoples, whose primary reality is "living on Indigenous land."

There are two ways Second peoples can engage with Indigenous peoples in the theological task. The first is to consider how Indigenous spirituality might shape the way we speak about God and the gospel. The second is to engage with social and political reality and what this means for faith and theology. It is this latter task that is my concern.

---

2. For readers who wish to explore further and in different ways the nature of theology, see Hall, *Professing the Faith*, particularly the introduction; or Migliore, *Faith Seeking Understanding*.

3. Hayes, *Toward Theology in an Australian Context*.

4. Goosen. *Australian Theologies*; Kelly, *A New Imagining*, and "Whither 'Australian Theology'?"; Lilburne, "Australian Theology," and "Contextualising Australian Theology"; Malone, ed., *Developing an Australian Theology*, and *Discovering an Australian Theology*; Pearson, *Faith in a Hyphen*; Wraight, *Contours of an Australian Christology*.

The Entry Point for Theology in This Place

Theology always begins in the experience of the theologian. That is, it begins in the life of one who is shaped by one's own context and experience in such a way that one takes particular questions, perspectives and concerns to the task, even as one seeks to move beyond those individual concerns. It begins with the social location of the theologian, who she or he sits with, and whose voices are privileged. Do theologians sit on the margins or at the heart of empire? Whose interests do they support and protect, and what is named as normal? For Second peoples the problem, as Sharon Ringe says, "is that our own social location among the privileged muffles the images of liberation, so that we fail to be grasped by them, or else we recognize only those dimensions of the images that do not threaten us."[5] Some voices are never heard, and in our world that usually means the voices of women, black people, people from Asia and the Pacific and Latin America, those who are poor, or those who are gay and lesbian. In Australia—and this is the central issue of this book—it can mean the exclusion of the voice and experience of Indigenous people. It is important, therefore, to acknowledge our own starting points and interests, and to hear voices that are not always heard.

I touched on my social location in the introduction, but let me add a couple things that readers should be aware of as they consider what follows. I grew up in a Presbyterian family, so have been immersed in the Reformed tradition with its concern for God's sovereignty, providence, and grace, and with an awareness of human brokenness. I live in a country whose modern European history was shaped by the Enlightenment and a sense that God—if God exists—was the absent clock maker. It is easier in this place to think of fate than providence. The university drew me into issues of justice—land rights, peace and disarmament, feminism, gay rights, the anti-apartheid movement, AIDS, human rights, and Palestine. These were not simply issues of justice but questions about God, Jesus, and the nature of the church. I found my mentors in liberation theology and in black and feminist theologies. For me the central question is, does it make any difference, this believing in God? Where could God be in these struggles and, particularly, in places of suffering and death and violence? How could one speak of God? If God is not where the church has sought to put God, where people have

5. Ringe, *Jesus, Liberation, and the Biblical Jubilee*, 14.

claimed God to be, does God have an abode that makes any difference to life? That is, the fundamental issue for me is not God's existence but God's presence and God's activity. I am a white male who grew up in a working-class home, but who has too often been in touch with and lived too easily with the centers of economic and political power. I do not easily move to the edge or see my "normal" for what it is.

Encounter and Location

To talk of God—to enter the theological enterprise—we must encounter God somewhere (even if it is in God's absence). There is a danger in this search to encounter God that it can be idolatrous, for we set the place, and seek to draw God to our place. We name God's place and restrict God to that place and do not allow either for God's ability to surprise or for the experience of others. In a real sense, that is what Indigenous people accuse the church of—seeking to determine where God is and avoiding the place where God is to be encountered in their spiritual life and history.

Yves Cattin claims that for the people of Israel, the covenant was the place of encounter with God. It was an encounter of love, and mercy between God and God's people. The covenant has at its heart the torah—the ethical obligation to justice to one's neighbor. It is in the practice of torah that one encounters God in the life of those others who are met in this practice. One encounters God in an act of human freedom that is also the practice of justice.[6]

The claim of the Christian faith is that the definitive location of God in the world is Jesus Christ in his humanity and place in history.[7]

---

6. Yves Cattin, "The Metaphor of God," in Duquoc and Floristán, *Where Is God?* 61–62.

7. Dietrich Bonhoeffer has taken up this issue of the location of Christ in the world as the central issue in Christology. He sees that the christological question not as, "how?" (which the ancient church asked) or as, "is revelation a fact?" (which modern theology since the Enlightenment has asked), but as, "who is Jesus Christ" (*Christology*, 33)? His answer to this question, using structural, sociological language was that who Jesus is, is always known in terms of "where" Jesus is in the world. The question, "who are you?" implies that one can encounter the person that one questions. Thus it is really the question, "Who is present and contemporaneous with us here" (*Christology*, 45)? It is not a question of Christ's being present in his power. He is present in his person, and the question is, "How are we to conceive of this presence so that it might not violate the wholeness of his person" (*Christology*, 45)? Bonheoffer's concern was to talk of the way

The true temple of God is the body of the crucified and risen one (John 2:21). This does not mean that this is the only place where God is encountered, but this is the definitive encounter, the one through which we make sense of all others. Jesus says that the way we continue to encounter him is in the lives of others, in the neighbor newly defined, and in the most forgotten in society (Matt 25: 35–46). This does not mean that people are God, but that through human beings God is manifested in the world. This encounter does not occur in every relationship, but where the relationship is a particular relationship of justice and mercy in which the otherness and humanity of the other (their life and story and experience) is respected, and in which they are not things at our disposal. It is this ethical relationship that is the metaphor of God. What Jesus made clear in his ministry was that the neighbor was the one who was excluded, ignored, rejected, and treated as an alien. The central New Testament affirmation is that Jesus is the one who is at the edges, outside the city gate, with the outcastes and socially excluded. Jesus doesn't talk about the people who are most often excluded as if they were charity cases but shares their meals, enjoys their hospitality, and insists on giving them priority in his life. Jesus builds relationships, listens to people, asks questions and respects answers, and speaks about God from the place of those for whom the promises of God do not seem to be working. As Luke 15:1–2 says, "he mixes with sinners and eats with them."[8]

We see a good example of this in Luke 7:36–50, where Jesus is invited home to have a meal with a Pharisee named Simon. The meal is disrupted by a woman who bathes Jesus's feet with her tears, dries them with her hair, and pours ointment on them. In that social context, it is outrageous behavior that suggests she is a woman with quite loose morals. Simon is horrified that Jesus would allow a sinful person to touch him, or that he would be in a place where sin and shame resided. Jesus teaches Simon about gratitude and acknowledgement of sin, and gently rebukes him for not giving hospitality to Jesus (and thus, in the

---

that Christ is perceived to be present in the world and to constitute reality. I explain this position more fully in "A Response to Aveling's 'Dietrich Bonhoeffer.'" Clive Marsh also develops this theme of identity and presence in *Christ in Practice*.

8. Risatisone Ete explores this issue of Jesus located on the edge of society—in his case, Samoan society—in "Christ the *Vale*," in Pearson et al., *Faith in a Hyphen*, 80–88. Mary Pearson adds a helpful dimension to this issue of presence with her article, "Where Is He Now? A Christology of Absence and Presence," also in Pearson, et al., *Faith in a Hyphen*, 118–26.

process, for failing to find the hospitality of God). "We encounter God's work—as the biblical witness already knew—primarily at the points where God descends into the 'utter depths' of life, where people need help the most and are most oppressed and where God resists the power of exclusion."[9]

I want to suggest that the location of Jesus in Australia is found in the sort of suffering that marked his death on the cross (suffering as loss of meaning and personhood, not just physical pain), in his being with the most marginalized and powerless (with those taken from parents, imprisoned, homeless, without work, wagging school). He is on the edge, in conflict with the empire (and often the church) that is at the centre. Jesus is always located with those whose land was given by God, but who have been dispossessed, and whose dispossession is therefore an act of unbelief. In short, he is present with Indigenous people as they struggle with the impact of invasion and continuing marginalization. As the Rainbow Spirit Aboriginal Elders say, "Christ who suffered on the cross continues to suffer with the land and the people of the land. In the suffering of the land and the people of the land, we see Christ suffering and we hear Christ crying out."[10]

The temptation for those who open themselves to the possibility of an encounter with God in the life of the other is to make the "other" an isolated individual, to ignore the place of the other in relationship and community, and to turn what should be acts of justice into welfare for one person. A relationship of justice needs to be a challenge to the structures of oppression, not simply care for one person inside those unjust structures. For those of us who are Second peoples, the encounter with God requires a change of social location, a genuine conversion from power and privilege to the ability to share life with those who are marginalized. It is the need to move from asking how we remain moral and Christian in an unjust society, to asking how we make an oppressive society just. It involves what Susan Parsons calls "taking care." To take care here means to understand oneself and others to be woven together in a network of relationships, and to keep these relationships sturdy and flexible enough to sustain us.[11] It means that we don't simply relate

---

9. Rieger, *God and the Excluded*, 176.

10. Rainbow Spirit Elders, *Rainbow Spirit Theology*, 67.

11. Parsons, "Redeeming Ethics," 212.

accidentally to the other, using them as instruments to encounter God, but that we must enter genuine relationships. In those relationships, and as we encounter God, we are constituted as people who together bear God's image in the world.

This claim that Jesus is the best revelation and place of encounter with God leads necessarily to a Trinitarian, communal understanding of God. To be a people who believe that God is one, and yet to proclaim that Jesus is the Son of God, means we must deal with the mystery of unity in diversity in the life of God. Jesus Christ is not, as some people claim, an equivalent term to God. That is, it is not right to say, "Jesus is God." God is more than Jesus, although Jesus is part of the Trinitarian life that is God. Thus, while Jesus may not easily be equated with the rich wholeness that is God, Jesus is the most perfect revelation we have of the life of God. The importance of this is that the God that we encounter is always communal, relational, and seeking to draw humanity into the swirling, dancing life of God. The God we meet is always Father, Son, and Holy Spirit, the one who creates, redeems, and sustains human life and hope. To be made in the image of this communal God is to be not simply an individual, but a people who reflect God's life in the world. And that God is named this way means that God is always mystery, even when we briefly encounter God. There is no guarantee that we will meet God as we serve another, no capacity to demand that because we have fulfilled certain requirements, God should be there (indeed to do this would be to treat the other as a tool, and not as others. We meet God through the grace of the Spirit. And the God we meet is the ever-moving Three-in-One whose life is a never-ending and ever-changing dance. We cannot stop that dance and say that this is what we mean by God but can only be drawn into the dance by Christ and know that we have encountered a mystery that is God.

To speak of the location of God in Australia is to move beyond a conversation about people to the idea of "country." It is not simply to sit with people in a particular political or social space but to honor the network of humanity and world that is country. That is, seeking God in Australia forces the theologian to enter the growing conversation about ecology and God's place in the earth. In Australia, though, the conversation must challenge the too-easy dichotomy between anthropocentrism and ecocentrism, and recognize the deep interrelationship and mutual need of people and country, a web of connected life in which one meets the Trinitarian God.

In the European narrative, earth is turned into "landscape" (something seen from outside and from a distance, as separate from us) and "real estate." It is a place ordered by straight lines and fences; it is packaged and divided into towns, factories, prisons, reserves, and places for churches. We may enjoy a place and may find identity in the nation or culture that occupies the place, but not in the country. For Aboriginal people there is no such separation of earth and people. Country is not simply where people live, but who they are. As Ambelin Kwaymullina says: "As Aboriginal people, we are a living, breathing, thinking physical manifestation of our land—a thread in the pattern of creation . . . Country is not simply a geographical space. It is the whole of reality, a living story that forms and informs all existence."[12] The land is not real estate but mother, father, sister, brother, and family. It/she/he does not exist apart from the people who care for and nurture it, neither do the people exist apart from their country.

The invasion of this land was an assault, not just on Aboriginal peoples, but on all life in country. Invasion destroyed the nurturing connections, ceremonies, and presence of the people. Invasion disordered country because it removed it from its own story and defined it within the story of the invaders.

To seek to encounter God with Aboriginal people is to question the way we impose a story that stops this place being country. It is to ask how Christians who honor the Holy Spirit found within the Trinitarian God can also honor the Spirit of this living land. Can we meet God in this "country"? Can we know and honor God's Spirit in this place, and listen to the voice of "country" as we do our theology? Can we see afresh the way Christ reconciles all things to himself (e.g., Col 1:17; Eph 1:10)? Can we discover new ways of expressing the tension between transcendence and immanence that allows God to be in, with, and under the world (panentheism), and explore sanctification in a way that involves, as Moltmann says, "integrating ourselves once more in the web of life from which modern society has isolated men and women and is separating them more and more"?[13]

12. Ambelin Kwaymullina, "Introduction: A Land of Many Countries," in Morgan et al., *Heartsick for Country*, 9.

13. Moltmann, *The Spirit of Life*, 172.

The Reformed tradition to which I belong says that God is revealed in Jesus Christ, who is the Word of God, in the Scriptures, in the preaching and hearing of the word, and in the sacraments. In beginning with God, made known in Christ, who is known in the neighbor, I am not trying to abrogate that claim; neither am I trying to downgrade the central importance of the biblical witness. I am simply trying to begin with what is often ignored—the encounter with God that comes in the other and in this country. All the sources of encounter are crucial. They each add to the possibility of whatever inadequate knowing is possible by human beings. They each act to question and offer boundaries to the other forms of revelation, and they open up ways of knowing that asks the other to be more open. For example, we know from Scripture that Christ promises to be known in the lives of the least, but we only have that encounter as we sit with the other, and act justly. As we sit with the other, we see things in Scripture that we were blinded to by our social location among those who are privileged.

Theology, Religion, and the Social Location of the Church

Before proceeding further in this exploration of a contextual theology, I need to briefly consider two historical movements that have played a major role in the shaping of modern theology. The first is the way we understand the nature of the religious life, and the second is the social location of the church. They often form a quite unconscious basis for theology, a part of the way our world is constructed, and an accepted norm that I wish to challenge.

The Nature of Religion

The theological task over the last couple centuries has been significantly shaped by the way the modern world has understood *religion*. Cavanaugh and others have pointed out that for a combination of reasons—the rise of the nation-state, the colonial designs of European nations, the Industrial Revolution and the split of the private and public, the Enlightenment challenge to religious knowledge and revelation, and the turn to the self as the centre of the world[14]—*religion* has been significantly reframed over the last four hundred years.

Prior to the Reformation and the Enlightenment, the term *religion* referred to the concrete ritual obligations that people owed to their God, and to the way of life that was implied in that relationship. Religion was not a separate category of life alongside family or politics or economy, but the public and social overarching narrative and ritual in which one lived all of life. Religion was understood as a virtue, as a set of habits and as character that was inescapably grounded in the communal life of the church. Theologians did not have to prove that it was reasonable to believe in God. Rather, their task was to show how people's belief in God was actually related to what was happening in their lives and the wider world, and how what was "natural" and what was "revealed" were mutually illuminating.[15] From the sixteenth century we have the gradual evolution of religion as a separate category of life, something that is distinct from other dimensions of human experience. Religion is no longer a particular social form of existence, but a set of common moral truths that individual people can discover rationally, and which apply to their personal lives. Religion became less a set of practices and the integrating ritual for the whole of life, and more a set of intellectual beliefs. It becomes a set of privately held beliefs, personal convictions that exist separately from one's public life and the practices of daily life.

This tendency to privatize religion was given impetus by the Enlightenment claim that all reality is known by reason, and that that there can be no place for revelation. Those who sought to defend religion from this attack did so on the basis that religion was found in a common human impulse, where all religions have a common core, discoverable by reason. To be religious no longer required a religious institution or a necessary integration between belief and life, but discovery of the best way to express one's own religious desires. Those who remained with organized religion tended to reflect the systematizing bent of the nineteenth century so that religion became a matter of propositions, intellectual assent, and tracts that defined the essence of true religion.

14. Cavanaugh, "A Fire Strong Enough"; Asad, *Genealogies of Religion*; Linell E. Cady, "Loosening the Category That Binds," in Brown et al., *Converging on Culture*.

15. I owe this insight to Hauerwas, *With the Grain of the Universe*, 26, a point he makes in relation to Aquinas.

Religion became something one believed in terms of propositions, and that fits with normal human reasoning.

The turn to propositions and tracts was not the only response to the Enlightenment challenge. A second response involved a turn to the self and religious experience. Rather than seeing religion as a set of propositions to be believed, this response held that feelings are the heart of the religious life. Religion is a category of experience, "understood as a distinctive, autonomous, immediate experience, prior to the concepts and beliefs that expressed it."[16] What is known about God is found in the human experience, what is often called the feeling of absolute dependency. What we experience about God has a clear correspondence to who God actually is. Faith is concerned for the "depth" in human life. Theology begins in the concerns of the human person and builds on the immediate relationship between experience, and what God is like. What is important in this understanding of theology is that the basis for our knowledge of God is the general human sense of God, and our need of God. Theology no longer deals with history and God's place in history but with God's place in the inner life of the individual. Theology becomes a way of giving expression to feelings and experiences, and tells the story of the self who is the measure of what is true, and who is in control of life.

The Social Location of the Church

It is generally claimed that the control of the state over all parts of life arose because the religious wars that followed the Reformation proved that the ecclesial authorities were incapable of providing peace, and the state took on this task. William Cavanaugh, on the other hand, argues that far from it being the religious wars that necessitated control by the state, what occurred were conflicts that grew from the state's desire to secure absolute control over their subjects. He argues that if the state was to claim absolute allegiance over people's lives, then religion had to become a set of privately held beliefs that had no essentially communal shape.[17] The individual has the complete freedom to think and believe

16. Cady, "Loosening the Category," in Brown, et al., *Converging on Culture*, 27.

17. Cavanaugh, "A Fire Strong Enough." Elsewhere he says: "By 'state' I mean to denote that peculiar institution which has arisen in the last four centuries in which a centralized and abstract power holds a monopoly over physical coercion within a geographically defined territory" (*Theopolitical Imagination*, 10).

what he or she likes, provided that in public one does nothing that disrupts the peace of the nation and the power of the sovereign.

The state no longer cares what religious beliefs people hold in private, and religious diversity can be tolerated—indeed encouraged—as an expression of personal freedom and individual choice. Religious tolerance is acceptable because freedom and individualism are key narratives, because people have become primarily citizens who are loyal to the state in all things, and because religion is reduced to interior beliefs and moral behavior. In this process the church is redefined as a free association of like-minded individuals, an invisible spiritual body rather than a necessarily concrete social community where Christians learn the practices that make them Christian. The church is allowed a place within the overarching reality that is the state in order to support people's primary loyalty as citizens and the existence of the democratic state, and to provide private morality.

The impact of the nation-state was also reinforced by the emergence of the modern industrial society. As the industrial society emerged, there was a shift from home-, craft-, and guild-based economies and social relationships to a situation where people worked away from their homes for wages. Life was split into the public and the private, and in the process women were largely relegated to the private area of life. As a social institution, the church was given a place in the public arena as temple (bearer of the communal story and of rituals that marked life's passages), but people's faith (increasingly an issue of personal confession) was made part of the private realm of the home. The church became increasingly concerned for personal morality and citizenship rather than for major theological issues—concerned for a morality that was often confused with middle-class manners and civilization. As discipleship was overshadowed by citizenship, and the church was told it had no truth that could be argued in the public domain, theology became about the church and personal morality and about the study of texts. It largely abandoned the public domain. Without being conscious of it, the church and its theologians have largely located themselves with those who possess power and influence and live within a world constructed to explain and justify that sense of power. Conversations about wealth, power, and the nature of the church, the understanding of salvation, and the place of ordinary people in the purposes of God are subtly changed by this location.

I believe that properly understood, theology points towards the location of God. It reminds people where they should be, what other voices they need to hear, where they are to be located if they are genuinely to be disciples. One of the challenges for theology is to reclaim the essential priority of discipleship over citizenship, of a radically obedient life over the need to sustain and protect an essentially liberal political and economic life as if this was the same as the Christian life. Theology needs to speak to the church again, not as a voluntary association of people but as the body of Christ, an elect community whose discipleship is a sign of God's intention for the world. And it needs to relearn the art of speaking with and to the wider world.

Habits and Practices

I share Archbishop Rowan Williams's understanding that the Christian life is not simply a lifestyle choice in a world obsessed with choices made in a marketplace. Rather religious life involves placing oneself in an environment in which people are "supplied with a set of possible roles within a comprehensive narrative, a set of possible projects shaped by the governing story."[18] Rather than being about assent to propositions and about privately held beliefs that are disengaged from the public life of the individual and community, a faithful life has to do with daily practices that are integrated into character, and with the way Christians enact the biblical script as an act of solidarity with Christ. The aim of life is to act in accord with the story, to show by one's life what is most true, and to enable the story to be seen in that life. Freedom, the archbishop reminds us, is not about my ability to do what I like, to be free from restraint, but is freedom from unreality, illusion, and the claim that life is shaped by other than God. That is, religious life is not simply about what we believe but is also concerned for the habits of human life and for the actions that seek to give shape to people's understanding of God, and God's place in their lives. Religious life is concerned for what is the just way we respond to our neighbor. It is about the practices that mark our life.

"By 'Christian practices' we mean *things Christian people do together over time to address fundamental human needs in response to and in*

18. Williams, "The Spiritual and the Religious."

the light of God's active presence for the life of the world [in Jesus Christ]."[19]
Practices are about the way we give expression to faithfulness through
the contours of our ordinary life. Practices are not simply individual
actions, but are things which arise in communities, and which pass between generations, while at the same time being flexible and capable of
change. Practices are founded on the wisdom of all people and not just
the "experts," and arise from the way ordinary people seek to live their
lives alongside and with other people in their community in the light
of their faith in God. Christian practices emerge within a realization
that human beings are caught in the dynamic of fall, sin, and grace and
that life must cope with many obstacles caused by human failure and
unjust social structures. Even Christians, who seek to follow Christ and
reflect his image in the world, bear a history of activity—racist, sexist,
violent, oppressive—that does not reflect the active presence of God in
the world.

The Christian Life as Drama

I would like to develop this claim about practices further by exploring
the image of religious life as the performance of a drama, play, or musical performance; a drama that is about relationships, belief, ritual, and
values; and about our way of being in the world. As I implied in the
previous section, in the last few hundred years people have begun to
believe that religion is either a play put on in our home that has nothing
to do with the real drama elsewhere, or a reading of the script of the
play. It has to do with an intellectual understanding of the play, an ability to discuss the characters and the plot. It puts us in the role of literary
critics, rather than people who actually perform the play. But religious
life is properly about taking up a role, learning the part, and entering
into the drama. To change the image, religion is more like playing a
musical instrument than it is learning music theory. In theory we learn
the notes, the scales, the different kinds of chords, the different timings
and rhythms; but none of this really matters until we put our fingers to
the keyboard or our lips to the reed of the clarinet, or until we pick up

---

19. Craig Dykstra and Dorothy C. Bass, "A Theological Understanding of Christian
Practices," in Volf and Bass, *Practicing Theology*, 18. The definition is from an earlier
work they coauthored, and the addition is a suggestion they make in a footnote (italics
original).

the drums and hammer out the beat. And practicing on our own isn't the goal either. The goal is to play with others, to blend our parts, to develop harmonies, and to share in the creation of the whole.

The Christian life is like that. We read the story, we worship together and retell the drama, we explore moral issues, and we read the lives of saintly people in order to form habits of life. We live out the Christian life, and in the living we learn more and change. It is like learning the clarinet. You actually learn to play the clarinet as you play it. You can learn the fingering and be told about the way your mouth touches the mouthpiece, but to play, you simply have to play. To be a Christian, you have to start acting like one. We develop habits and patterns of life, and we form a character, a way of being in the world, that allows us to respond to new situations.

Sometimes our performances of the Christian drama are straightforward. At other times, people are able to challenge our performance because they believe we have distorted the text by a reading and performance that excludes them from the story or that claims one part of the story as the whole. At other times, though, we are faced with issues for which there is no straightforward text, no easy part for us to play. It is at those times that we understand the very point of all the hard work that lies at the heart of the Christian journey. That is, Christian discipleship is in part about learning the story, developing habits of life, and incorporating practices into our life in ways that they become second nature. These practices are not simply about the formation of individuals but are the way the church is formed, and restored constantly to life, so that it can be the place where people learn the art of being Christian. When we are confronted by challenges and new things, we have so embedded the story in our life that we can act quite naturally out of our character and improvise a way forward. We learn the tradition so thoroughly that we act from habit in ways that are appropriate to the circumstance, and in ways that embody the wisdom of the tradition. Neither are our actions totally new, nor are they simple repetitions of the past.

The easiest way I can think about improvisation is with jazz. When we listen to a person improvising, it may appear that one can simply play what one likes, making up things along the way. But improvisation is a much more difficult task, for the musician who is improvising is bound by the chord structure played by the other musicians and by the need to bring the piece "into land" at the right stage, creating and releasing points of tension. The improvising musician has by endless practice learned patterns of notes that fit both the chord structure and the pattern of the music, and out of that deep sense of what has been learned is able to improvise appropriate music.[20]

"Improvisation [in the Christian life] is concerned with discernment. It is about hearing God speak through renewed practice and attending to the Spirit through trained listening. It is corporate, since it is concerned with a group of people acting and reflecting like a theatrical company. It is concerned with engaging with the world."[21] Samuel Wells reinforces this point about improvisation with his claim that a common misunderstanding of improvisation is that it is about being original. The aim is not to be original but obvious, to act out of the long period of learning that has formed one's character and virtues. To be obvious is an act of trust in the script and of our small part in a drama that is much bigger than us.[22]

Improvisation is inevitable for a people who seek to discern God's presence and action in the world, and who do not simply wish to live rigidly by the text of Scripture or tradition (i.e., to repeat the past). Scripture, tradition, reason, experience, and people who model the Christian life provide the boundaries, the chord structure, the written script of the play; and we then embody that grace in our lives in fresh ways.

What Does This Conversation Suggest about the Task of Theology?

How do we conceive of the task of theology as Second peoples who occupy Indigenous land, who are committed to a sense that God is encountered on the margins of life, and who are aware of the privatizing of faith and of the way citizenship shapes theology? Let me indicate quite briefly what sort of theological process I am suggesting.

---

20. Samuel Wells has a very helpful account of improvisation that is based on the theatre. See Wells, *Improvisation*. He reminds us that what we are seeking to do is to place what is actually happening to people within the larger drama of God's actions in Jesus Christ, that the way we judge our performance is by the sort life that is lived, and that we need to understand that we are part of a multi-act play where we are responsible for neither the beginning nor the end but only our part.

21. Wells, *Improvisation*, 66.

22. Ibid., 67.

Hopefully the model will be clearer in the last section as we pick up on particular issues.

Theology, as I understand it, is based on an understanding of religion and faith that has to do with the whole of life. Religion is not a separate, private thing. It is not simply about private belief or individual morality or some private religious experience. Religion, properly understood, is not simply about texts and propositions; neither is theology about the exposition of such texts. Nor is religion simply about human experience, with theology as the way we explain how Christian faith gives a particular expression to this general human life. Christian faith is about the performance of the Christian story; it is about practice, habit, and character. Ultimately it is about innovation or improvisation.

Rebecca Chopp reminds us that theology is a form of testimony rather than simply a form of rational discourse. In speaking of the poetics of testimony, she challenges the idea that witness and testimony are things to be judged by modern theorists, be they theologians, historians, or philosophers. Witness speaks of suffering and hope; it offers the voice of those who are often ruled out by rational discourse and judgment. Poetics "seeks not so much to argue as to refigure, to reimagine and refashion the world."[23] Witness and testimony do not listen to the other to judge them but to hear their claim to existence, and to speak on their behalf to question the claims of the priority of reason in the face of the centrality of "reverence for life."[24]

Theology is part of the social construction of worlds and a means of cultural critique. Theology provides some of the significant language, symbols, and myths that explain and shape the world, and the theologian needs to be aware that these are culturally and historically relative. That is, the images that any Christian community or individual Christian has available from the very broad pool of images will be shaped by denominational history; geography; social class; institutional considerations; attitudes regarding gender or race, or regarding what is described as heresy; historical circumstance; and social situation.[25] What is being challenged in this book is how the available images of the saving work

23. Chopp, "Theology and the Poetics of Testimony," in Brown et al., *Converging on Culture*, 61.

24. Chopp, "Theology and the Poetics of Testimony," 63.

25. Ringe, *Jesus, Liberation, and the Biblical Jubilee*, 8–9.

of Jesus and the nature of the church have been limited in ways that distort the relationship with Indigenous people.

Theology speaks of what people consider to be sacred, opens up new understanding of that sacredness, and questions the idols that people use to support their power and lives. The very speaking of theology is itself an important agent in any struggle, a means by which the search for liberation can occur. The task of theology is not to close down the conversation about reality, to end the contested struggle about meaning and identity, but to provide ways in which the conversation can occur. It is to help people engage the many partners that are part of the theological conversation, not so that there is no position taken or truth claimed, but so that even as we make claims about truth, we recognize that we can be wrong. We engage with others to challenge and push the boundaries of what we claim to be true. As Samuel Wells reminds us, one of the tasks of theology is to reincorporate those who have been lost from the Christian story. It is to reweave into the story those people and events that have been forgotten, rejected, suppressed, and hidden (like massacres, stolen children, and deaths in custody).[26]

Theology is essentially a set of marginal notes that help people perform the Christian life. Theology is an exploration of the Scripture, tradition, practices—the words and performances—of the church in order to provide models, comments, and mentors who enable people to perform the faith. The aim is a faithful performance, one that embodies the intention of the story in this place. My claim is that in Australia, we will neither read the text rightly nor enact the play properly without we have sat with Indigenous people, and allowed them to shape our enactment and be part of the play.

How Do We Actually Go About the Theological Task?

The first task in theological reflection is to clarify what issues are being raised and, in the process, to ensure that we hear the voices of those who have most at stake, and who are least likely to be heard. I want to know what happened, and how the event is placed within people's world of meaning and understanding of faith. What I am trying to identify is what is at issue—theologically. That is, what in this situation of human living and struggle is being raised about God, God's relationship to

26. Wells, *Improvisation*, 162–64.

the world, and the nature of the church's confession of Jesus Christ?[27] I listen with suspicion to the telling and describing of those with power, of those who can determine what is normal. In this regard theology is often the task of making claims explicit, bringing to light that which shapes people's lives but remains unstated and unowned.

Imagine the theological tradition as a landscape. The second step is to enter and explore that landscape. One of the things that the notes in the margin seek to do is to introduce people to this landscape that is the Christian tradition. At different places on the landscape we have the wisdom of the church about issues like God, Jesus, the Holy Spirit, the church, Scripture and tradition, or the virtues of the Christian life. Individuals approach this theological landscape from within their own context and with their experience and issues. They need to decide where they will enter the landscape, for that will greatly influence the way they approach other parts of faith, and the weight given to them. For example, the issue of sexuality and leadership changes depending on whether our entry point is the nature of God, the meaning of salvation, the nature of humanness, the form of the church and its leadership, or the authority of the Scriptures.

Christians enter and then move through the landscape, one guide after another—one part or other of the tradition—pointing them in a different direction. The theological tradition offers companions to accompany them on their journey. They are offered directions, suggestions about major landmarks, and advice about the way different parts of the landscape are related. They hear the advice critically, asking questions and checking whether such wisdom does help their journey. Within this task will be an attempt to listen to the voices of those who raise questions about the tradition and its tendency to oppress them, who question the way I have read the tradition, and who seek to bring to the surface parts of the tradition that have been suppressed. They see connections to other themes and topics, and move into different conversations. So, for example, in asking about sin and injustice, I want to ask about the nature of human life and about the Trinitarian God's intention for human life. If I ask about suffering, I want to ask about the nature of the sovereignty and providence of God, which raises ques-

27. Neil Darragh talks about this in terms of pivotal questions that articulate the issues in ways that can be addressed to Scripture (Darragh, *Doing Theology Ourselves*, 52).

tions about the suffering of God in Jesus Christ, and a theology of the cross. If I ask about marriage, I want to ask about Christian vocation, the shape of Christ in the world, the role of the church, and the general and special providence of God. The issue is, which part of the theological landscape does one engage as a partner in contextual theology, and how does that part of the landscape interact with other parts and shape the way into the whole? How we arrange our theological framework, the sort of doctrine or areas of theology that we use to draw our map, is crucial. For example, do you treat Scripture as a separate doctrine and allow things like tradition to find a bit part in that conversation, or do you locate Scripture within the topic of revelation (part of the discussion of how one knows God)?

Two of the dangers in theology are, first, that people's context and experience are not taken seriously, and that they are not allowed or able to question, challenge, and engage with the wisdom of the past in ways that bring them genuine life and wholeness (the complaint of feminists and black people, for example); and, second, that people only know a narrow part of the landscape. This narrowness occurs because each tradition has its own map (and thinks that this is the only map), and each local community has its own slightly amended version of the tradition's map. This way of doing theology, of locating issues within the landscape, of finding our way across the landscape only works if theologians have taken the time to understand the various contours of the theological tradition, and their interconnection. There is a need for theologians to read widely so that they have as many entry points, or connections as possible for the experiences, and situations they are facing. This is the crucial task for us and grows from an assumption that is well expressed by Hall: "We who profess the faith *here* and *now* are persons who have been brought into a long tradition, one that existed for centuries before we arrived on the scene. A conversation has been in progress and we, who have entered the room late in time, are obliged to listen carefully if our own contribution is to be pertinent."[28] Thus an important part of theology is to be clear about the conversation into which we have stepped, and to make our contribution to the ongoing conversation in the light of the wisdom we find in that tradition and in our context and experience.

28. Hall, *Professing the Faith*, 33.

The third task is to suggest what this conversation between context, experience, Scripture, and tradition says about a rereading of faith, and a renaming of the practices of the Christian life. It seeks to name where it believes God in Christ is present, with whom and how, and how this new belief and practices reflect that claim. It speaks of the place where the church is located, and how it is called to reflect on that location.

Theology is a form of social action and a way of living. It seeks to offer people wisdom about the way they encounter God. The issue for theology in Australia for Second peoples is that we need to re-locate ourselves if we are to encounter God and do theology. We need to be located in those diverse places where Indigenous people sit, not simply as curious people or helping people, but as those who respect the other and seek to act with people in the pursuit of justice and mercy. We need to let go of the assumption that God can be encountered completely in our places, and to be open to new ways of hearing and new ways of understanding where God is.

Issues in Contextual Theology
God, Justice, Church, and Relationships

Introduction to Part Two

IN PART 1 I HAVE SOUGHT TO EXPLORE THE CONTEXT WITHIN WHICH Second peoples in Australia need to think about Christian faith and to do theology. I have also suggested a particular understanding of theology and a model for going about the task of theology.

In this part I want to see how this model might actually work as we speak about four specific issues: whether we can speak of God in a way that matters; the relationship between order and justice in the purposes of God; the signs that a community actually is the church; and the challenge of reconciliation, covenant, and treaty to present relationships.

Each chapter in this part is structured in a similar way. Each begins with a particular contextual challenge. In chapter 4 this is a clash of worlds: the Enlightenment, invaded space, and the Indigenous world. Chapter 5 begins with the Intervention of the federal government into Indigenous communities of the Northern Territory. Chapter 6 begins with two stories that challenge the nature of the church. Chapter 7 simply tells a little of the history of three challenges to present relationships in Australia.

The second section of each chapter in this part is an exploration of some parts of the tradition, a brief consideration of the theological landscape. Clearly we never draw on the whole of the tradition when we do theology, but we choose those parts that seem to speak to our immediate concerns. I have chosen an entry point into the tradition that was suggested by the story or event in the first part. The third section of each chapter in part 2 seeks to offer some theological comments about what this conversation between event and tradition might mean to the theology of a Second people.

There are some core claims that lie behind the chapters in part 2. First, faith is not simply about intellectual assent but is a way of life. Second, theology is contextual and therefore takes seriously people's experience both as a place where they encounter God, and as a source of questions for the tradition. Third, Indigenous people are not the objects of this study, but subjects who keep challenging what we assume and know. Fourth, a central challenge for the church is its social and theological location and the need to question the way it shares in racism and oppression.

Samuel Wells speaks about the importance of reincorporation, "in which discarded elements in the drama are woven back into the story."[1] This is a word that can describe the way Jesus in his resurrection is woven back into God's story. Reincorporation is about reintegration of diverse strands of people into the community. This book is an attempt to enable Second peoples to be open to the reincorporation of Indigenous people back into the story of the land.

There are two dangers in the church's desire to reincorporate Indigenous people back into its life and story. The first is that people will not really be reincorporated but simply managed on the edge of the church, tolerated in ways that still manage and control people's place in the church. The second is that the church will operate with a liberal philosophical view of justice that says everyone should be treated the same way. With the best of intentions, an effort is made to include those who have been previously excluded. Individual liberty and place are extended to everyone. But there is another way of seeing—one that suggests that those who have been excluded are not simply seeking an equal place in a life determined by those who already have it, but are presenting the challenge of an alternative model of community. They are asking not simply to be included but for the church to change, and the danger here is that the church will not be able to let go of its belief that the church, as it is, is "normal." They want to weave people into the story, but do not want them to have any influence on the story, or for the story to change. The remaining chapters challenge us to change.

1. Wells, *Improvisation*, 13.

4

Does God Actually Matter?

Introduction

THE AIM OF THIS CHAPTER IS, IN THE LIGHT OF THREE CHALLENGES
to the way we speak about God (invasion and suffering, a culture that
finds little space or need for God, and the claim of Indigenous people
about the presence of God in this land), to see if we can draw from the
tradition helpful insights to talk about God as one who matters. By asking whether God "matters," I mean that life is different because of God,
and that we are not, for all practical purposes, atheists. I am not seeking
to offer a definitive response to the challenge that is posed here, but to
question some parts of the tradition and to suggest some of the contours that need to be followed as this conversation develops further.

The Challenge to the Way We Speak about God

God and the European World at the Time of Invasion

While a case may be put that those who went to the U.S.A. did so in
search of religious freedom and to establish God's colony, the world had
changed remarkably by the time the British decided to occupy Australia.
In Australia there was no question of God and promised spaces. This
country was to be a place to house those caught up in one of the great
movements of human life: the growth of modern industrial society and
the movement of people to the cities. This was the time of the emergence
of the Enlightenment, with its claim that all things could be determined
by human reason, that the world could be explained without God, and
that if God existed at all, it was as an absent clock maker who set things
in place and now sits at a distance watching with bemusement as the

world goes on. From belief in stability, order, permanence, and meaning, people in Europe during the nineteenth century came to feel that "all was not well with the world." There was a loss of a vital framework of values and beliefs, a feeling that life did not have any real meaning. The future became a thing of uncertainty, so that the present was lived as intensely as possible, or there is an escape into nostalgia and the desire for the Golden Age. Part of this unease was the growing sense of the secular, the sense that human life rests in the hands of human beings, and that people could no longer rely on assistance from a transcendent Being. Both survival and happiness became a human burden.

The Industrial Revolution created many of the circumstances that made escape from reality seem such a necessary act. Not only did it create the slums and gross poverty that marked the nineteenth century, it also contributed to the lack of meaning, which infiltrated the societal and individual consciousness. The sense of universal meaning and wholeness is particularized for most people in the meaning they find in their relationships and work. In work, in particular, people are able to give expression to their identity, relationships, and sense of worth. For working-class people in particular, industrialization and specialization removed any sense that they were creating something meaningful. They were simply selling the one thing they had to sell—their labor—in order to live. It was hard to see work as vocation, as an expression of Christian faith in their daily lives (particularly as many did not have that faith). This trend towards meaninglessness was worsened by the separation of the public and private spheres, which also marked industrialization. Alienation from work, and thus from a large part of each day and its activity, meant that life became disintegrated and divided, and lacked an overall meaning and wholeness. The great majority of Australia's earliest "settlers" came from the large cities of England, where this alienation was a mark of life. They brought to Australia a sense of meaninglessness that was rarely tempered by contact with any scheme of meaning provided by Christianity.

The church and community that came to Australia were also shaped by the Enlightenment. The Enlightenment saw a repudiation of the idea that human beings needed the tutelage of the church, and an affirmation that each person was in control of him- or herself. As I have explained in earlier chapters, in this period religion became a privatized and internalized reality, even if the church remained a more-

or-less important social institution. In this world, public debate was to be conducted without religion, and religion was a particular, voluntarily joined sphere of life. The church had a role "as legitimators of individualistic virtues and nationalistic values in secular states willing to grant 'religious freedom' in return for unthreatening ideological support."[1]

There is in the Australian community a deep sense of fate; a sense that if there is a God, it is a God who is distant and uninvolved in the world, and who is not concerned for human beings in their daily lives. That is, Australians struggle to talk meaningfully of One who is transcendent yet involved in human life. The response to this is large amounts of gambling, self-depreciating humor that mocks the world and its fate, a search for experience that fills the void of lack of meaning, and—as ANZAC Day celebrations or responses to the Bali bombings show—a deep appreciation of the courage of those who confront that fate. There is admiration for the courage that confronts the hand one has been dealt in life, the stoic acceptance of life, and the ability to get on without fuss.

Speaking about God on Indigenous Land

It is not easy to describe the heart of Indigenous religious life, that which has become known as the Dreaming. It is an understanding of life in which each of the features of the landscape, the markings of the world, is an "icon" of the presence of the Spirit of the earth and a promise that the Spirit is still present and animates life. That Spirit is also present in, and represented by the various animals and other life, which become totems or signs of people's place in the world. From this are drawn complex relationships, and the laws that govern life. That understanding is sustained by sacred story and by ceremonies that mark not historical events (e.g., the life of a political community) or seasons (e.g., the natural cycles of a farming people) but the boundaries and forms of life of people deeply attached to land.

Indigenous Christians believe that God placed them here, and gave them this land. God was already present in this place and did not need to be brought by the invaders. How then do they/ we speak of God who allowed/ purposed invasion and dis-location? What does the church

---

1. Mudge, *The Church as Moral Community*, 37.

learn from God's presence in this place, and how is God revealed? How can we speak of God and the sacredness of land in this place

The Meeting of Colonizers and People of the Dreaming

Conversations about God are also shaped by the history of invasion, dispossession, and ongoing marginalization. That is, Second peoples in this place are faced with one of the oldest questions in Christian theology—the existence of suffering in a world that is ruled by God. In this case, the suffering is not caused by disease or natural disaster but by human action and invasion, and the question is how such invasion, and the suffering it caused, fits into claims we make about God and God's providential care. How can one believe in God in the face of ongoing Indigenous reality? That is, if God is good, how did God allow for this land to be invaded, the people killed and oppressed by racism, and the people still forced to live on the margins? There is inescapable existential agony in this question.

The Tradition

To step into the theological landscape that is concerned for God is to confront issues about the nature of God, the language we use to speak of God, the way God is known, the mystery of the Trinity, God's place in creation and redemption, God and the end of history, and the meaning of providence and its relation to human freedom and responsibility. Within this wider range of issues, there are some parts of the tradition that are worth particular exploration. These parts are the providence of God, how we speak of God in the face of suffering, questions around natural religion and how we know God, the need for human beings to know God in human form, and the challenge of a theology of the cross.

The Providence of God

The traditional affirmation of the church is that God is Lord of, and offers providential care for, the whole created universe. God is not the absentee clockmaker but remains involved in creation and guides it towards God's desired goal. As John Calvin says:

> It were cold and lifeless to represent God as a momentary
> Creator, who completed his work once for all, and then left it.
> Here, especially, we must dissent from the profane, and maintain
> that the presence of the divine power is conspicuous, not less in
> the perpetual condition of the world than in its first creation ...
> After learning that there is a Creator, it must forthwith infer that
> he is also a Governor and Preserver, and that, not by producing
> a kind of general motion in the machine of the globe as well as
> in each of its parts, but by a special Providence sustaining, cher-
> ishing, superintending, all the things which he has made, to the
> very minutest, even to a sparrow.[2]

Calvin believed that all events were governed by God, and that there
could be no chance or capriciousness in life.

This affirmation of God's providence is most severely tested and
challenged by the reality of evil and suffering. Christians are confronted
with the question of whether they have to deny the reality of evil (a
profoundly difficult thing to do in our age), whether they can restrict or
alter the way we normally think about the power of God, or whether to
deny God's goodness. One of the issues raised by suffering is, does God
care? Indeed, can God feel suffering?

By the third century, influenced by Stoic philosophy and the value
of *apatheia* (being above passion or emotion), the church argued that
God, being whole, complete, and without need, could not suffer (this
is called the impassibility of God). This move to emphasize God's omnipotence and omnipresence over against God's compassion, longsuf-
fering, justness, mercy, and kindness had a political purpose. When the
church began to enter the centre of power as partners with Constantine
in the shaping of Roman power, there was no place for a suffering God,
or for a God who acted in solidarity with human beings. God was made
to be distant from the world, to act not in and with the world but towards the world from a distance. God was the one whose power sustained the world and underpinned the power of those who ruled. God
worked through representatives: kings who reigned by divine right, and
churches whose hierarchical form justified such a chain of power. The
attributes of God emphasized power, majesty, omnipotence, sovereignty, and the impossibility that God could feel or suffer (for this would
imply change and the possibility of real relationships between God and

---

2. Calvin, *Institutes of the Christian Religion*, bk. 1, chap. 16, para. 1.

people). God is removed from creaturely suffering and becomes the one who lives in unapproachable majesty. God is not only relocated to the political centre of society but becomes unapproachable and dispassionate. God emerges as the one from whom all tenderness is removed, the God of power and might, who requires the church to mediate God's life. As the perception of God changed, the practices of discipleship that transformed Christians into a kingdom people were spiritualized and came to have no real relevance to the political life of society.

Providence and Suffering

Within the Christian theological tradition, the issue of human suffering arises as, how can God be all powerful, and all loving, and there still be suffering (the problem of theodicy)? There have been essentially two schools of thought in relation to this issue: that of St. Augustine of Hippo (354–430) and that of Irenaeus of Lyons. (c. 130–c. 200). Augustine claimed that God created a perfect world, into which entered the sin of Adam, which was essentially the abuse of human freedom. Suffering is a symptom of sin. It is an act of punishment or chastisement, and is as a call to repentance. Irenaeus, on the other hand, said that the perfection of creation will not occur until the end of history. Suffering is a necessary part of human life through which human beings grow and reach their full potential and perfection. Suffering is both a symptom of sin and a mark of our life as a work in progress.[3]

There is a third part of the tradition, which does not seek to explain suffering but suggests that we must simply trust God because our knowledge of God is very limited. We must patiently endure suffering and not argue against it or challenge its existence.[4]

What these three views hold in common is the belief that God is responsible for suffering. God has the power to control the world and everything that occurs in the world. God has power over nature and the affairs of all people. In this understanding, the main characteristic of God is not love, wisdom, or saving work, but power.

Daniel Migliore provides us with a helpful understanding of some other voices that are emerging in theology. He speaks of Karl Barth's

---

3. See Dutney, *Playing God*, 68–69; and Migliore, *Faith Seeking Understanding*, 123–25.

4. Migliore, *Faith Seeking Understanding*, 123–24.

concern for providence that is interpreted in the light of a christocentric and Trinitarian faith that allows God to preserve, accompany, and govern the world while providing space for human agency and freedom. That is, his doctrine of providence is shaped less by assumptions about omnipotence and more by his understanding of grace. The issue that needs further work in Barth is the relationship between God's actions against evil and the work of human beings, and the relationship between patient acceptance of evil and active forms of protest.[5]

Migliore also explores "protest theodicy" (a challenge to the total goodness of God), "process theodicy" (God's power is radically restricted and is expressed persuasively rather than coercively), "person-making theodicy" (as Irenaeus says, evil and suffering help people to grow into what God intends them to be), and "liberation theodicy" (people are called to share in God's redemptive suffering and struggle against suffering in the world).[6]

One of the important questions posed by the tradition is whether we can speak about God without speaking of God's absolute sovereignty, of God's control of the world? If we do not or cannot speak of God's sovereignty, does this mean that, for all practical purposes, we live as atheists, people without God? The issue is, what do we see as the necessary divine attributes; in what do we ultimately put our trust? And, connected with this, what criteria do we have for the set of attributes?

For Christians, the criteria are christological. The attributes of God are those we see in Jesus Christ. While we believe that God is in the entire world, the pain that is in the world stops us from a too-easy equation of God with the world. There is far too much that makes no sense and that contradicts the human search for humanness and wholeness. We know there is a huge gap between God and our reality. But as Christians, we claim that this gap, this temptation to agnosticism and unbelief, "is interrupted by a Word once spoken, by one life lived and death undergone."[7] It is not the case, as some christological debates seem to assume, that we know God from other sources and have to figure out how Jesus could be God, and what attributes Jesus adds to our understanding of God. Rather, we begin with the claim that it is in

5. Ibid., 125–28.

6. Ibid., 129–31.

7. Lash, *Theology on the Way to Emmaus*, 156.

Jesus that we have the clearest revelation of God, and this christological claim, linked with our Trinitarian understanding, changes the way we understand "God."

Andrew Dutney suggests that we can continue to speak of God, and even of God's power, but in a different way. God's power is not power that interrupts life occasionally, but is continuous and sustaining power through which all life is made possible. It is enabling power that cooperates with life, and makes freedom possible.[8] Dutney seems to be opting for a response that is very close to what Hubert Locke sees as the liberal understanding of the way God acts in history. Locke says that in both liberal and evangelical theology, God is seeking to redeem the world, but the issue is whether this occurs by the way the righteous change structures, or the way God changes people's hearts. "In the context of the Exodus story, for example, liberals see God as empowering the children of Israel so that they overcome the oppression of slavery. For evangelicals, God changes the heart of the Egyptian pharaoh so that Pharaoh frees his Jewish slaves."[9]

Stanley Hauerwas suggests that the problem of suffering does not challenge our belief in God, but rather challenges the way we speak about God, the story we tell. It forces us to ask where God is in this suffering and, thus, how we can speak of this God. We are not asking, can we talk of God? "but rather what kind of God it is Christians worship that makes intelligible our cry of rage against the suffering and death of our children."[10] We are not seeking intellectual understanding. There is no hope if all we gain is new information and learning. Rather, as Hauerwas says, the only hope we will have is if we can place alongside our stories of pointless suffering a story of suffering that shows we have not been abandoned.[11]

Involving himself in a discussion with Walter Brueggemann, Hauerwas raises a couple crucial points. First, questions about theodicy became acute in Israel when this people, who were in a covenant relationship with God that seemed to promise them a great place in

---

8. Dutney, *Playing God*, 83.

9. Locke, *Searching for God in Godforsaken Times and Places*, 31. I don't find his division between *liberal* and *evangelical* helpful, but the general distinction in positions seems helpful.

10. Hauerwas, *Naming the Silences*, 35.

11. Ibid., 34.

the earth, are sent into exile. There is a deep challenge to the assumption that good people prosper, and that evil people suffer. Theodicy is never just a question of God's relationship to evil but is also about social arrangements of access, benefit, and the way God is named in that arrangement. So, second, questions about suffering arise in particular power structures and reflect that social situation. When we pose the question of theodicy as a universal one, we obscure the major issue of the situation and experience of the one who asks. Questions of suffering are always asked by particular people in particular times and places. It makes a difference if the person is suffering, causing the suffering, or pretending to turn a blind eye to the suffering. Third, theodicy legitimates the way society is organized, for the very language of theodicy speaks of power and of who has access to that power and of whom it protects. Abstract theories of theodicy, separated from real human struggles, concentrate on explanations. They explain why suffering exists, and why the world order is the way it is. They make suffering an issue about God's relationship to suffering. They allow human beings to take charge of the world, because clearly God cannot deal with suffering, and humans must.

Finally, to return to Augustine and Irenaeus, the important issue is that they were not trying to provide an explanation, a metaphysical explanation, for suffering but were suggesting how people should respond to suffering (with either repentance or growth). For them, history had an importance, a place in which the work of God is revealed in Jesus Christ. Their response to suffering had to do with how they would be church, God's people within God's history. The church does not have a solution to the problem of evil or for how to speak of the providence of God in the face of suffering, but is a community that sustains life in the face of that which would destroy it.

How Can We Speak of God in Indigenous Life?

In an earlier chapter, I suggested that in the Reformed tradition there is an understanding that God is known and is revealed in Jesus Christ, the Word incarnate, as well as in Scripture and through the Holy Spirit. I suggested that we meet Jesus in the least and most marginalized in our society.

A significant issue for the church in Australia in the face of the claims of Indigenous peoples about the presence of God is, to what extent can the church acknowledge truth about God in Indigenous spirituality, and religious and social life?

This question raises in a particular way the more general questions of what place a plurality of religions have within the purposes of God, and the place of Jesus Christ within that plurality. This is a major issue in the twenty-first century, particularly in the present context of terrorism, conflict, and war. In Australia we need to make sure that this important conversation does not exclude or overshadow the question of God and Indigenous peoples.

There are a variety of positions taken within the Christian theological tradition in regard to other religions. These range from "all truth is in the Christian faith, and other religions are totally in error" to "all religions are equally capable of revealing God and offering salvation," with various positions in between.

There is no space to deal fully with what has been and continues to be a complex debate. I simply wish to suggest that conversations about God in Australia need to take seriously the claims of Indigenous people, and to offer a couple of suggestions for a framework for that conversation.

First, it is helpful to distinguish between what we can know of God in other religions (the issue of revelation), and whether other religions are a source of salvation. This issue is important in Australia; for if I understand Indigenous Christians correctly, they are suggesting that God has been revealed among them, and they have God's law to enable them to live faithfully with God, but salvation is found in Jesus Christ.

Second, I agree with Barth that our knowledge of God in other religions is not simply a claim about the ability of all human beings to understand God by reason. God cannot be known this way, by what may be called natural religion, but can only be known through revelation and the Word of God, who is Jesus Christ.

Barth doesn't provide a simple definition of the Word of God, probably because the Word, like God who speaks it, cannot be easily contained. Essentially, though, it is the Word that God "*spoke, speaks, and will speak* in the midst of all men."[12] This Word of God is preached,

12. Barth, *Evangelical Theology*, 22 (italics original).

is written in the Scriptures, and in its fullest form is revealed in Jesus Christ. There are not three Words of God, but it is one Word that meets us in these three interrelated forms. Central to this understanding of the Word of God is that it is revealed by God as an act of grace, it is not what we discover for ourselves. There is no general knowledge of God that people can come to on their own; revelation actually seeks to rescue people from their own idle imagining. This leads to Barth's critique of the claims of natural theology: "Natural theology is the doctrine of a union of man with God existing outside God's revelation in Jesus Christ."[13] Natural theology assumes that people can know God apart from Christ, as if people were equal with God and could know God. "By way of natural theology, apart from the Bible and the Church, there can be attained only abstract impartations concerning God's existence as the Supreme Being and Ruler of all things, and man's responsibility towards Him."[14] That is, there is no way for us to know God who is known in Jesus Christ, and his salvation, apart from revelation.

Third, in his later writings Barth claims that the Word that is heard in the church in Scripture and preaching, and which is the source of the church's life, is found outside the church.[15] The church is a more narrow sphere than the whole of creation, which God rules and desires to save (1 Tim 2:4), and so "we cannot possibly think that He cannot speak, and His speech cannot be attested, outside this sphere."[16] That is, Jesus Christ can create witnesses well beyond the sphere of the church. When the church hears these words, it "can find itself lightened, gladdened and encouraged in the execution of its own task."[17]

The *Basis of Union* of the Uniting Church in Australia was, through its drafters, influenced by both Barth and Bonhoeffer. It gives a great deal of emphasis to Christology and the identity of Jesus as the Word of God. For example, paragraph 4 says, "Christ who is present when he is preached among people is the Word of God who acquits the guilty, who

---

13. Barth, *Church Dogmatics: A Selection*, 51.

14. Barth, *Church Dogmatics*, IV/3: 117. Barth speaks of "natural religion" in *Evangelical Theology*, in various parts of *Church Dogmatics*, and most important, in *Knowledge of God*. Hauerwas reflects on Barth's work on natural religion in *With the Grain of the Universe*.

15. Barth, *Church Dogmatics*, IV/3: 114–34.

16. Ibid., 117.

17. Ibid., 115.

gives life to the dead and who brings into being what otherwise could not exist." It is also open to Barth's comment about the Word's existing beyond the church. For example, it says in paragraph 11: "In particular the Uniting Church enters into the inheritance of literary, historical and scientific enquiry which has characterised recent centuries, and gives thanks for the knowledge of God's ways with humanity which are opened to an informed faith."[18]

It seems to me that when the church in Australia seeks to speak about God and particularly as it speaks about covenanting and the particular place of First peoples in the church, that it explores this insight in the tradition about the Word outside the church.

Revelation as Personal Life

Barth's reference to the threefold revelation of the Word of God that is revealed most fully in the human life of Jesus Christ suggests that, as Migliore says, "only revelation through a person can be fully intelligible to us, who are persons, and only personal revelation can adequately disclose the reality of God, who is supremely personal."[19]

Yet as central as the revelation of Jesus Christ is, we need to at least tentatively question this claim, and what it implies about the places where God is present and revealed. The doctrine of the Trinity suggests that while God is clearly and centrally revealed in Jesus, it is not possible to describe Jesus as an isolated individual as we often assume in Western culture. God is community, and the true reflection of God's image is the social existence of human life. In some way Jesus is social existence. Indigenous people claim that, for them, it is never possible to understand the person apart from the community or from country.

In Richard North Patterson's novel *Exile* there is an important conversation between an American Jewish lawyer and his Palestinian lover. She is trying to explain why she cannot marry him. She says to him that he is an individual, complete in himself, obligated to no one, and able to satisfy whatever desire he has. She, on the other hand, is not simply an individual. She is defined by family and culture, and the fact

18. See, Uniting Church in Australia, *Basis of Union*, 7, 10. I am grateful to Damien Palmer for drawing my attention to this connection between paragraph 11 and Barth's thoughts on the Word beyond the church.

19. Migliore, *Faith Seeking Understanding*, 35.

that she is a Palestinian. She lives inside a culture of shame (not guilt) that is concerned for image, name, and honor. To marry is a decision of the family, not just herself.[20]

Granted that Jesus is a personal revelation of God, does this not have to mean more than just the individual and personal life of Jesus? Is there not something about relationships and country that makes him who he is? That is, is the revelation in Christ not just God crucified but God who is the Word in creation, inexorably related to the earth? Is not the comment about the need for a person to reveal God to persons too narrow in its conception of humanity?

The Crucified, Suffering God

Drawing on the work of Martin Luther and Jürgen Moltmann, Douglas John Hall explores another part of the tradition around providence and suffering that has to do with the way love and power are part of the character of God: a theology of the cross, as opposed to a theology of glory. A theology of the cross begins with the assumption that God's primary desire is that there be free creatures, and that the world be preserved and redeemed. The issue is not whether God has power or could not use this power, but what exercise of power, what relationship with human beings, will achieve this goal. A theology of the cross begins in the purpose of God in creation, and in the incarnation, as a critique of the idea of God as the *deus ex machina* who rescues us from the things we cannot solve ourselves, including finitude and death. It affirms that God desires to be our God and wishes for us to be God's people. The only way in which God can achieve God's purposes is through the power of suffering love, through a providence that works within the movements of history rather than being imposed on them. God is one, as Hall reminds us, "who is obliged by his own love to exercise his power quietly, subtly, and, usually, responsively in relation to the always ambiguous and frequently evil deeds of the free creatures; a God who will not impose rectitude upon the world but labor to bring existing wrong into the service of the good; a God, in short, who will suffer."[21]

A theology of the cross begins in incarnation. The very idea of incarnation is concerned for embodiment in a particular time and place.

20. Patterson, *Exile*, 119–21.
21. Hall, *Cross in Our Context*, 87.

We have tended to treat the incarnation of Jesus as a moment or point in time in his life and divinity. We have treated humanity as flesh, blood, and bone, and thus the concern is how Jesus could be born as a human being (the Christmas event). Yet the incarnation is really about Jesus being fully human and, thus, is about the sociocultural and political particularity of Jesus's life. It is about what Luther described as God's "deep sympathy with human weakness and wretchedness."[22]

Any discussion of the work of God needs to begin with the principle of divine unity, at least in the sense of the unity of God's work. That is, there is a mutuality or interdependence of being or action of the three persons of the Trinity. Whatever is done by one person within the Trinity is done by all, and each person reflects the others (see John 10:28–38). For example, if we speak of the "suffering" and self-emptying of the Son (Phil 2:5–11), this must also be taken as a claim about the totality of God's being. In 2 Corinthians 12 Paul says, "My grace is sufficient for you, for my power is made perfect in weakness" (v. 8). He was speaking not just of the comfort we could find in Christ in the midst of human struggle and weakness, but of the way God is present to humankind.

A theology of the cross presupposes a church that shares in God's suffering in this world. As Dietrich Bonhoeffer says, the church is called to sustain itself as a human community immersed in the world, identified with struggle and suffering, finding our identity not in being religious but in being there for others in God's suffering.[23] The gospel of the suffering God suggests that the church is not above the world but is deeply immersed in it. We are to live unprotected, in dialogue with life, engaged in and by our context, and participants in God's suffering in the whole of life (not just religious life).

Does God Matter in Australia?

Can a Second peoples' theology find any real assistance in the tradition to deal with the particular way in which the question of God arises in this country? I believe so, and would like in the remainder of this chapter to suggest some marks, or contours, of such an ongoing theological conversation.

22. Ibid., 21.

23. Bonhoeffer, *Letter and Papers from Prison*, 279–82, for example.

Claims and Worldviews

The claim of the Enlightenment world is that everything can be explained without God. It also claims that truth is largely to be equated with facts, and that facts are discoverable by observation. In the face of these claims, the church has often abandoned the field in regard to God, and has made personal, inner experience the measure of religious truth. Or, alternatively, it has insisted that the claims of the Christian faith can meet the criteria for truth set by the modern, secular world. The liberal part of the church accepts the definition of truth offered by the physical and social sciences (including history), and commits itself to reassessing all its own claims. The conservative part of the church accepts the criteria for truth, and then involves itself in discussions about the way the account of creation in Genesis, for example, meets that criterion (and so involves itself in debates about the teaching of creation science in schools).

I suggest that any discussion about God in Australia needs to engage in a more contentious way with the claims of science and the modern/postmodern world. The scientific worldview is just that: a worldview that has been socially constructed to explain the world and protect interests. It does helpfully explain some aspects of the world, and has led to many insights into the world, but it is not the only way to see the world. It is not the only way to understand truth. The church needs to question the way socially constructed worlds become absolute fact, so that it opens the way for conversations about other realities.

I think God matters because the story of suffering and broken relationships is part of a bigger story about reconciliation, and the future reign of God. These events are not simply part of a self-contained human history and life but must be placed within God's world and God's future.

The Location of God

The question of whether God matters is tied to the issue of God's relationships and social location. To whom does God matter? is an important part of the question. I argued in chapter 3 that God is primarily found in Jesus, who is in turn found among the poorest and most marginalized. Social location has to do with, among other things, the issue of meaning. That is, is my suffering and dispossession simply about so-cial forces, or is it part of the will of God?

When we speak about God in Australia, we speak of one who is first of all among the poor and marginalized, and whose very presence challenges the language of the church. I think God matters because by God's presence, and through the witness to that presence in Scripture, God says that those often seen as the least are valuable and significant. God sits with people to offer them not simply comfort in the midst of suffering, although this may be the case, but the courage to struggle against ongoing oppression. God matters because God calls forth a church that, although it can get things wrong and still wears a legacy of being in the wrong place in society, can call society to a better place and sit down with others.

The challenge to those who do theology is that they speak not from a distance into the life of suffering, but out of a sharing with people and God. Theology speaks not just *about* God but *with* God in the world. To speak of God in Australia is to be challenged about where we are located, and what this does to our speaking. It is to ask ourselves what it means to speak of a despised and rejected Savior, and what it means to be the church of such a Savior. It is, I would suggest, to live with an *ecclesia crucis* that is based on a *theologia crucis* (a theology of the cross) rather than on a theology of glory.

God and Invasion

God matters in Australia because God refuses to allow us to call inva-sion good, not so we are always guilty, but so we don't too easily make it part of our history. It is to recognize our history as broken, violent, unbelieving, and unfaithful and to own that ambiguity in relation to Indigenous people. The gospel community ensures that we do not for-get the past.

European society since the Enlightenment has worked with a view of endless human progress, even in the face of disasters and suffering that should have challenged such a worldview. It is a view of progress that owes much to Hegel's suggestion that progress occurs through a dialectical process. That is, progress occurs first through one action of event, then through its opposite and then through a synthesis of the two. The important issue is that progress continues, moving along towards a more perfect end. And because all history is moving forward in this way, then suffering becomes just an unfortunate footnote, or cost that must be accepted. The belief was that Europe was on the leading edge of the economic development that was so crucial to this progress. This justified colonial expansion and invasion, and provided a cover for the suffering of Indigenous peoples. Their suffering was one of the unfortunate consequences of progress, a small thing within the bigger picture.

This view of progress also underpins the sense people have that the world is essentially a good place where all issues that confront us will be solved by technology and human ingenuity. As Douglas John Hall suggests, this was (and generally still is) a society sustained by a sense of optimism that represses all sense of despair and misinterprets the nature of Christian hope.[24] There may be moments of sadness or even death (though hidden away in our lives in ways that avoid its reality, or made so public in the media that death is just another TV drama), but everything will be all right. There are still things to buy, wealth to accumulate, more sex to experience, and life to be lived.

When evil actually does confront us, when we are forced to face what we seek to avoid, we are clearly surprised. What we have done in Australia, though, is to hide the historical reality of suffering if we can, and if we cannot, to refuse to believe that suffering arises out of evil. Invasion and suffering (and present-day attacks on land rights in places where mining could happen) are the unfortunate necessities of inevitable progress.

One of the difficulties, of course, is that having banished God and evil from our world, we have no categories to deal with evil. Part of the ability to do theology as Second people in this place is the willingness to name the pain, suffering, and horror in our history, and to stop making excuses or justifying what occurred as the actions of well-intentioned people. The reality is that whatever the intention, far too much occurred in this place that was contrary to the heart of the gospel of Jesus Christ. Colonial suffering, death, and destruction are a reality around the world. Millions upon millions of people died to make way for European expansion into the Americas, Asia, Oceania, and Africa. We must name suffering in this place and allow that suffering to shape our theology, or

24. Hall, *Bound and Free*, 56–58.

our agenda will continue to be shaped by the history and experience of Europe. To do that, we must believe that God cares about this suffering and how we name God, and where we find God must reflect God's response to this pain.

What I am suggesting in this chapter is that a major contribution of theology by Second people is our willingness to name invasion and its consequences as evil. What occurred was not simply an unfortunate side effect of progress and European economic expansion. It was evil. And in case readers wonder, I am not simply talking about wrong human action, some moral failure. I am speaking about action that is opposed to God, action that undermines and disturbs God's desire for life and wholeness, and which harms God's image-bearing people in their communal and individual lives. The church shared in this evil. There can be no throwing of rocks by a pure and self-righteous church, but an honest naming by a church capable of repentance, change, and reparation.

Conclusion

It is beyond the scope of this chapter to consider how speaking of God is changed by a recognition that God was present in this place prior to European occupation. This recognition raises three important issues: where was God present, what does that reveal of God, and in what ways has God revealed Godself? That is, how has the Word, who is responsible for creation, and who is found most clearly in Jesus, also found in this place? In many ways, this is a particular example of the whole issue of God and other religions.

Finally, I suggest three areas of awareness as we seek to speak of God in the invaded place:

1. We need to be wary of too-easy speech about the providence and action of God, of language that suggests God is in control and ignores the sense of absence and fate that marks Australian life.

2. We need to reflect on the way in which the providence of God is expressed not just historically/politically on land that is seen as real estate or "promised land," but in the very form of the earth, the shape of the creation as "Mother" and "Spirit," and how this shapes human life and relationships.

3. We need to take seriously claims about God and oppression, and who God "sits with," and how we speak of oppression and liberation, and a God who "takes sides."

Dare we speak of God in Australia? Only if we speak carefully, tentatively, in a context of solidarity with those to whom we speak. Only if we can speak of a God of suffering who calls the church to earn the right to speak God's name as it is willing to suffer and name the way Indigenous people sit at the heart of God. Only if we can tackle in a more nuanced way than much of the Reformed debate about natural religion what it means for God to be known in this place. Only if we speak from within suffering and in relation to those who are marginalized, and do not simply offer words from a distance. It must be about God who joins with, sits alongside, and names reality so that oppression is recognized. Only if, in some way, the Word, the creative Word, is revealed here and has something to do with the people and the country.

5

Justice, Order, and Humanity

Introduction

This chapter is about justice and order, and sin, culpability, and freedom. It is about the way people are blamed and shamed, not for repentance and change, but for control and political advantage. It is about the nature of justice.

A Story: An Act of Intervention

In 2007 the Northern Territory (NT) government released the report *Little Children Are Sacred*. The report recognized that sexual abuse in Aboriginal communities is one consequence of the breakdown of Aboriginal culture and society, and results from the combined effects of poor health, alcohol and drug abuse, gambling, unemployment, poor education and housing, pornography, and a general loss of identity and control. It suggested that Aboriginal people are willing and committed to solving the problems, that existing programs need to work better and be coordinated in a more helpful manner, and that there needs to be funds and resources committed for the long term. The NT government sat on the report for quite some time and seemed unwilling to act.

On June 21, 2007, the prime minister of Australia declared the matter of sexual abuse in Indigenous communities to be a national emergency, apparently without consultation with the Northern Territory government or with Aboriginal people. A number of strategies were announced, and police and military personnel were immediately sent into communities to increase protection for children. Alcohol restrictions were introduced on Aboriginal land, all children under sixteen years were to have compulsory medical examinations (this was later withdrawn), welfare reforms tied income support to desired social behavior (e.g., attendance at school, meals at school), and the federal government took control of townships and land.

None of these measures was found in the recommendations of the Northern Territory report. Some actions (for example, extra policing for six months) contradict the report's recommendation of increased policing in the long term. Of the eight recommendations relating to alcohol, none suggested banning alcohol from Aboriginal communities, mainly because this would simply shift the problem to other communities where alcohol is available. Some important recommendations in the report (for example, the community-justice process) received no response at all.

There is no question that there is poverty, poor housing, abuse of alcohol and other drugs, physical and sexual abuse, and inadequate funding support, policing, and justice systems for communities. The normal systems of a community, which allow powerful and abusive people to be held accountable, did not appear to be working, and there were few outside systems that could get past the gate keepers (often white) who protected abusers and kept the communities isolated. There were few processes in place to protect the women and their income from men, which meant that money was diverted from food and care of children to gambling and alcohol. Women often welcomed the intervention simply because of the income management that was introduced, although, overall, people were ambivalent or opposed to the intervention.[1]

The central issue, the one around which most debate would implicitly revolve was, given this reality, and particularly the lack of power for women in communities, was the best response an intervention that took away some rights (like control of income, and permits in towns), or should there have been a process that enabled people to take control of their own lives?

Three Voices That Offer an Explanation

In what follows I wish to present three responses to the intervention— Marcia Langton, an Indigenous, feminist academic and activist; the

1. See, for example, the Central Land Council briefing paper: *From the Grassroots.* The report grew out of a listening tour and series of community consultations.

Uniting Aboriginal and Islander Christian Congress (UAICC); and the media—in order to see how they have understood the meaning of what occurred.

Marcia Langton

Langton supported the intervention because of the widespread abuse, because of what she saw as the protection of powerful and abusive men, and because she believed the intervention would protect women and children. In her analysis she makes the accusation that there has been decades of failure by different levels of government to respond appropriately to the needs of Indigenous communities. Some of this was due to the way in which governments simply did not use funds as intended, and spent far less on issues like education in Indigenous communities than they did in other communities. She suggests that the failure of previous governments made the intervention inevitable.[2] She reminds us of how difficult this situation of abuse had become, how widespread and horrible. Action could no longer be avoided, and the situation no longer left in the hands of the very people who perpetuated the violence. Nor could inactivity be defended in terms of Indigenous control—because the children and women who were being abused had no control. To speak of self-determination and control where there is none, is to continue the abuse.

Langton said that the media had used Indigenous suffering as a kind of visual pornography. The crisis became a public spectacle in which real suffering is parodied for political purposes. She suggests that some of the analysis of this issue has relied on a position that needs perpetual victims for the analysis to work. It is axiomatic to most Australians, she says, that Indigenous people be poor, sick, and forever on the verge of extinction, rather than capable, economically empowered, free-thinking, independent people. This image of a people capable of taking an active role in Australian society "has been set to one side because it is more interesting to play with the warm, cuddly, cultural

---

2. Langton, "Real Change for Real People." This was an edited extract from her then-unpublished essay, "Trapped in the Aboriginal Reality Show," in *Griffith Review: Re-Imagining Australia*.

Aborigine, the one who is so demoralized that the only available role is as a passive player."[3]

She claims that one of the most disturbing features within Indigenous communities has been the failure of the European criminal justice system. There has been a seemingly ideological and racist (paternalistic) decision to not apply the law even in the case of murder or of the rape of children. There seems to be a sense of guilt for the conditions under which people live, and a refusal to hold people accountable. There is an implicit assumption that traditional men are worth protecting (when they are the people responsible), but that Aboriginal victims don't count as much as other people. There is also, I would suggest, a form of racism that thinks Indigenous people are sexually promiscuous (because they are more "primitive and natural") and do not suffer the same way. How else does one explain a judge's decision in a case of the rape of a ten-year-old girl that the girl had probably agreed to have sex with the nine men; how does one explain that the judge imposed almost no punishment on any of them? This judge's ruling has since been overturned. [4]

Like other major players in this situation, Langton is seeking to construe the world in a particular way. Together with Noel Pearson, whose Cape York Institute for Policy and Leadership board she chairs, she is concerned to construct an understanding of Indigenous identity as independent, strong, able to participate in society on equal terms, and not victims. Pearson argues that it is unhelpful to blame society, historical factors, or contemporary dysfunction for things like addiction, even though they may make people more susceptible. He says that the real factors are the availability of substances, money to buy them, time to use them, examples of other people who use them, and a permissive ideology in relation to use. That is, says Pearson, abuse of drugs is the problem rather than, as some claim, the thing that causes wrong behavior.[5] The implications of these comments are that people need to take responsibility and be accountable and stop blaming other social forces.

3. Langton, "Real Change for Real People."

4. Ibid., 31.

5. Noel Pearson, "Drug Abusers Should Just Say Sorry." Pearson is here talking of Australian Football League stars and drugs, but it is the same philosophy he applies to Indigenous communities.

As a black feminist, Langton has a critique of male power and of a male telling of how the world is, reminding us that it is not just the marginalized that are of concern but the most marginalized. She also implicitly critiques any desire for a romantic portrayal of Indigenous society, and draws quite sharply the issues of power, brokenness, and abuse. She is seeking a realist construal of the world, meeting a need to deal with abuse as pragmatically as necessary.

The Uniting Aboriginal and Islander Christian Congress

The UAICC suggests another way to see the intervention. They were opposed to this sort of government action because of lack of consultation, and the failure to involve the community in finding answers to its own problems. It is a response that is less immediately pragmatic, and more concerned for long-term solutions of self-control. It is also more suspicious of government motives (e.g., opening the place to mining), and more aware of the way such bodies have acted in the past in areas like the stolen generation. Among the central issues raised in a combined letter to the church from the UAICC and the national director of Uniting Care on November 13, 2007 were consultation, upholding the NT Land Rights Act, and the need for Indigenous people to control their own lives.

We should be careful not to throw this position into too sharp a disagreement with Langton's position. There is a concern for what is happening in communities, and a particular concern that women feel safe, and that family structures are protected. The issue is that intervention simply passes responsibility to other people again. Intervention does not help people engage in developing relationships and processes that hold people accountable, make them responsible, and force them to rectify wrongdoing. The need is for a form of intervention, based on consultation and support for local leaders (women and men) who can rebuild respect for law, boundaries, relationships, and accountability.

This position recognizes the brokenness of human lives and community but challenges the liberal theological view that wants to ignore sin and blame circumstances for everything. This position recognizes sin; understands the way people's lives are distorted, broken, and limited in their choices; and still calls them to be responsible for what they do. It challenges the Protestant polarization of law and grace, and recognizes the place of law in social life (whatever the issue in salvation), because we need to be nurtured into the way we live.

The Media, Free Speech, and Protection for Whom?

There is one other group that particularly interests me in this conversation: the media. There were important commentators who supported the intervention and, in particular, the decision to remove the permit system, because they believed permits stopped them doing their job. Their argument was that if the media had been able to freely enter these communities, then this abuse could not have been covered up by powerful men. They are raising issues about power, secrecy, and who controls information and for what purpose.

The media were construing a world where freedom is an ultimate value, and where they can be trusted to be independent and fair. They are claiming a benevolent media and the normalcy of the way they see the world. They wanted to position themselves as the only group without ideological interests, other than an interest in freedom of expression and the power of truthful telling. For example, Nicholas Rothwell says: "No reporter committed to press freedom could support access permits, which are granted by land councils, and function to ensure favourable media portraits of communities and the powerbrokers who control them."[6] The Opinion column in the same edition of the *Australian*, in speaking of the permit system, says, "The checks and balances that protect the individual in mainstream Australian society were removed. There were few if any police, there was no media scrutiny and almost no chance of independence through education or economic opportunity."[7]

I think there is some sense in this argument in a context where there are few other ways to scrutinize behavior, including the behavior of police, white bureaucrats, and powerful men. What journalists ignore, however, is that the things that a dominant society takes as normal and, more importantly, protective of their interests, are often experienced by minority peoples as quite contrary to their interests and place in society. The reality is that the media do not just report the news or shine a light on what is happening. How and what they

6. Rothwell, "No Time for Dreaming."
7. "Time to Permit the Truth to Be Told."

report actually helps to constitute what is considered news. And the images that the media has portrayed of Indigenous people throughout our history have frequently contributed to racist stereotypes. This isn't a value-free exercise, and the suggestion that maybe it is, and that the media is simply doing everybody a favor further reinforces the view that other people know what is best for Indigenous people, and how we report thing is what is "normal."

What each of these the positions raises is the issue of how a community manages power, order, responsibility, accountability, and justice, and how it answers the question, whose order and whose justice?

Another Way of Construing This Event

Any analysis of this situation needs to be very aware of the dangers of assuming that all Indigenous people share the same views, or that there is a single Indigenous identity. We need to be aware of the relational and ideological assumptions we make when we choose which voices we will privilege in these sorts of conversations. Why are we willing to hear some voices and not others; and what part of our own agenda is being reinforced through that choice? There is the danger of ideological analysis, of seeing everything through a single lens that may have to do with the politics of the Left or Right. There is the danger of an overly simplistic analysis, one that wants all the evidence to stack up on one side, rather than one that sees this as a multifaceted and contested issue.

I believe that the best way to see this issue is in terms of loss of order, and the response of those at the centre to such loss of order through the imposition of their own order. This occurs within a framework of racism and shame.

Abuse and the Loss of World Order

Feminist analysis reminds us that sexual abuse is about power more than it is about sex.[8] In his analysis of the sexual abuse of children, Alistair McFadyen also suggests that the abuse is not about sex. He says,

---

8. I think this insight is right, but we need to also recognize that *sexual* abuse of women is a particular site of power and abuse, one that is particularly focused on gender and hierarchy. That is, sexual abuse is a different kind of abuse with a different meaning than, for example, physical assault.

"abuse seems to be a means for resolving issues of personal identity that reflect distorted identity structures sedimented through histories of distorted interaction. Whilst the means of resolution have become sexualised, neither they, nor the issues being so resolved, are intrinsically or specifically sexual. Issues concerning security, trust, worth, vulnerability are resolved through power, domination, humiliation or the semblance of intimacy."[9] For this reason it is difficult to see why the existence of pornography has become such a focus in the intervention, other than that the sexual-abuse–pornography link places responsibility on individuals and connects with the often-moralistic streak in liberal/conservative politics.

I believe that individual acts of abuse are often the acts of people without meaning, hope, control, place, or value. Abuse is a way of expressing deep rage against others who have less power, within a narrative of hierarchy and male domination. Without denying the wrongness of what has been done, and without implying that the sin does not matter because of the abusers' own suffering, we need to take seriously the issue of shame. It is the shame of people who have no meaningful role in their community, no dignity, no sense of control over their world, and who feel they are the subject of social derision. It is shame that renders people socially dysfunctional, warps self-image, and weakens people morally and spiritually. It can lead to disgust with the self, to a sense of inferiority, and to a sense of being isolated and left alone.[10]

While most reports of Aboriginal culture until relatively recently described a hierarchical society reflective of European society, recent research by women suggests that the male writers found what mirrored their own experience rather than what traditional society was actually like. According to this analysis, Aboriginal society was relatively equal in terms of gender power and had ways for women to maintain that place in the society. Hierarchy depends on the concentration of ultimate (sacred?) knowledge in one place, and the dissemination of that knowledge/power through a hierarchical system of patronage and power sharing. In Aboriginal society there was no single locus of knowledge and power. Various persons (men and women) held different stories, and each person only had the right to tell that story and exercise authority

9. McFadyen, *Bound to Sin*, 114–15.

10. Park, *The Wounded Heart of God*, 83–85.

in relation to it. Each keeper of the story needed others to hold their stories in order to enable various story or song cycles to be completed.

Contrary to this, the very heart of the modern nation-state's form of governance is based on male sovereignty and a male-headed family, what Native American feminist writer Andrea Smith calls the "heteropatriarchal family."[11] The colonization of Indigenous people in this country has involved the colonization of gender relationships through missions, schools, the teachings of the church on gender and hierarchy, the distortion of scholarship, and the very structures of society.

If we are to understand the abuse in Indigenous communities, we need to see that colonization has undermined a largely equal gender relationship based on access to sacred sites and stories, and has replaced it with a hierarchical narrative that is also supportive of Western capitalism and the nation-state. The frustration for Indigenous men is that there is no place for them in this new hierarchical world, but there is a narrative that gives permission for the abuse that is always potentially present in hierarchical relationships. Abuse of children is able to occur because of the false construction of normalcy and because of secrecy. In order to be susceptible to being abused, children must be isolated from those who could take care of them. This means that abusers use physical and social power to remove children from the support of other adults. Often children are sworn to silence by threats (including the threat that they will be to blame for the consequences), and other adults are silenced also by—in these communities—fear of police, government intervention, the removal of children, or the disruption of their community.

In this new world there are few structures that can hold people accountable, that provide a system of rewards and punishments, or that give honor to those who make and enforce social standards and law. There is no expectation of accountability and responsibility, and no way to enforce such expectations even where they exist. And there are no real structures of protection, including police and the courts. As was made clear in chapter 1, the relationship between Indigenous people and the justice system has been fraught and abusive. The legal system has been used to keep Indigenous people in whatever place governments wanted them at any time. While white people might tell their

11. Smith, "Dismantling the Master's Tools," 94.

children, "If you are in trouble, go see a policeman," it is more likely that Indigenous people—given their history—would tell their children, "If you get into trouble, don't tell the police." Not only are there issues of power within the Indigenous community, there are issues of power between that community and the criminal-justice system.

Racism, Hiddenness, and Shame

The federal government's decision to intervene in communities in the Northern Territory was underpinned by an implicit racism of the kind suggested in chapter 2. That is, it was a racism that said Indigenous people had both too much and too little, and that knew that such public actions as the intervention would shame Indigenous people and remind them of their "place" in society.

One of the ways in which colonial domination is maintained is through actions that enforce a definition of the limited humanity of those who are colonized or who belong to the lower classes. These actions and their connected symbols and narratives provide a symbolic order that is crucial to social formation. Indeed, as Fernando Belo points out in his commentary on Mark, the various elements of a symbolic order (the values and norms which regulate social life)—e.g., the law—regulate the relationship between bodies and individuals in society.[12] Drawing on the work of anthropologist Mary Douglas, Ched Myers suggests that every society has symbolic systems that define and reproduce social power, maintain group boundaries through "taboos," and order the chaotic universe. These systems are reinforced by ideological discourse.[13] Myers develops this issue particularly in regard to "debt" and "purity," and honor and shame, and the way these support social inequality and exploitation. Honor has to do with social standing in society, and with whom a person may interact and under what circumstances. According to Myers, there were those in first-century society whose role it was embody shame (because they are outside the honor system) and thus to remind the community of its boundaries.

Anthony B. Pinn has a powerful account of the way various symbolic systems were used to restrict and define the humanity of slaves

---

12. Belo, *A Materialist Reading of Mark*, "Part 1: An Essay in Formal Theory."
13. Myers, *Binding the Strong Man*, 70.

in the U.S.A.[14] The aim of slavery was to transform black people from people to objects or property, through symbolic actions that remove Africans from the social tissue that provided meaning and humanness. Pinn argues that the auction blocks were used to create a sense that slaves were the objects of other people's history and were only bodies and chattel. "Through this ritualized manipulation of African bodies, new social arrangements complete with existential and ontological ground rules are put in place."[15] After the end of slavery, lynching was used to induce the same terror as the slave auctions, and to reinforce the idea that black people were are not adults, did not have control of their world, and were always inferior to whites. White supremacy was played out on black bodies through the terror and torture of lynching and imprisonment.

It is my claim that what Pinn calls rituals of reference, and what Myers and Belo call elements of a symbolic order, have been used in Australia to significantly restrict the identity of Aboriginal people. Indeed, the primary identity that has been forced on Aboriginal people, I wish to argue, is that of "invisibility." The invisibility was reinforced through colonists' refusing to make a treaty with Indigenous people; through the fiction of *terra nullius*; through colonists' denying having massacred Indigenous people; through colonists' denying Indigenous people citizenship, the vote, rights of residence, and the right to drink alcohol; through white Australians' taking Indigenous children; through whites' imprisoning Indigenous people at high rates; through whites' placing Indigenous people on missions, nearer to isolated areas. What is clear from the conversations and telling of stories that I have shared with Indigenous people is that many Indigenous people grew up feeling invisible—at school, when it came to work opportunities, and when people shared information on how to cope in society. This invisibility was a source of enormous shame. Part of the structures of invisibility was the desire by governments to "mainstream" services to Indigenous people, to act as if they were not culturally and socially distinct, but simply another part of the society.

Australian churches participated in the construction of a symbolic world of invisibility. Mainline churches had little contact with

14. Pinn, *Terror and Triumph*.
15. Ibid., 49.

Aboriginal people in more populated areas. They reinforced the view that "real" Aboriginal people lived a traditional life in isolated communities, and other people were not really Aboriginal people. Aboriginality was kept hidden.

In all cultures, invisibility always has the possibility of visibility, a forced visibility whose purpose is shame and the use of people for political ends. I think that, among other things, the action of the federal government in response to the report on abused children is an act of giving visibility for the purpose of shame and political ends. This is the point Marcia Langton was making about the emphasis on the pornography. In the way the government responded to the crisis, in the way it ignored the long-term recommendations of the Northern Territory report, in its refusal to consult Aboriginal people, it has continued the symbolic world of invisibility, except when people need to be seen to achieve an end.

One of the issues with invisibility and shame is the way in which people are named economically, as consumers; and the way in which they are ashamed because they cannot participate in this world. Our whole culture values people as consumers, as people with the ability to own, buy, and be famous because of their highly visible big-spending lifestyle. We beam this message into all communities, including Indigenous communities, and then make it clear that they have failed because they cannot participate in this world. And the message is that they cannot, not because the system fails, but because they simply are not good enough, do not have the skills, and are not properly human enough to participate (this message is given to all poor people).

Andrés Tornos reminds us that in most societies people bear the burden of their faults in a small social community of family, or among a small number of friends, "and it was they who confronted us with society's demands."[16] That is, those who reminded us or confronted us with criticism of our conduct were those who also shared our life and were concerned for our place in the community. These were voices from whom we could expect understanding, and with whom one could negotiate change and repentance and reparation.

Our society is different. The media now acts as the conscience of the community. It: bares our sins for all to see, and has no interest in

16. Andrés Tornos, "Guilty and Without Access to God," in Duquoc and Floristán, eds., *Where Is God?* 39.

us and our renewed place in the community. Our sin is simply a news story, and the voice that comes to us is one that finds moralizing quite easy. Now the point is shame and public punishment, with no thought to what happens to the people once the story ends. The partnership of media and political moral outrage played out on a very public stage can only lead to denial, defence, and despair, for there is no quiet, hidden, and silent space to face oneself, God, and change. The intervention was no friend confronting one with the need to change, and journeying along the way. This was the men who wanted Jesus's permission to stone the adulterous woman in a very public place (John 8:1–11). Where in this event is the space for conversion, change, and the rebuilding of human dignity?

Imposed Order

At the heart of what happened was the issue of imposed order. Those at the centre determined the nature of the order that should exist in Indigenous communities without providing any voice for the people to shape that order. As with many actions of control, the control of the body (through medical examinations, control of access to land, and control of money) is control of the body politic, and in this case simply replaced one form of bodily control with another.

Governments, those at the centre of empire, fear chaos, a lack of social order, and any behavior (including injustice) that threatens their sense of control from the centre. The historical pressure is always towards the centre. The desire was for control of the political agenda as an election drew near, the desire to control a crisis that could prove embarrassing. The federal government had seen decades of reports about abuse and had done nothing. Yet in an election year it turned this issue into a national emergency that justified significant intervention in Indigenous communities, and undermined the authority of the Northern Territory government in relation to Indigenous communities.[17] The order that lay

17. Alan Ramsey, "A Cynical Scratch, a Pustular Response," suggests that the knowledge of such abuse had been in report after report and had been consistently ignored by the federal government. In a further article on the same page, he says, "Howard's national emergency is a political one. He has an election to win. The genuine national emergency he is hiding behind is the one his Government has ignored effortlessly for 11 years. Just read the public record" ("The True Story of Inaction Is on the Record").

at the heart of the government's worldview had to do with possessive individualism and personal responsibility, the priority of the economy, assimilation and mainstreaming, and development of land. What the government needed, faced as it was by an election, was an issue that would showcase its ability to provide order in the face of chaos, fear, and the difference of the "other."

The intervention challenged the particular structures, and expression of hierarchy within deeply distressed and disadvantaged communities, and offered some short-term protection to women. It challenged the power of men with government power, but as an act of control further undermined the power of men and provided no way for women to find a more equal place in social relationships. The work of transforming social disorder and violence that has its foundation in shame needs more than this sort of action. It requires the slow action to transform the shame and violence-causing social order.

The Theological Landscape

Order and Justice

The first entry point into the theological landscape is the way the church has spoken of God's providential concern for order and justice. The issue is not whether governments have a role in providing such order and justice, but the relationship between order and justice. Those who are concerned for order always ask a minimalist question about justice: how much justice is needed in society to maintain the existing order? That is, what is the minimal change we need to make to quiet revolt and end protest? Those who are oppressed, on the other hand, ask what kind of order is compatible with the exercise of justice. The challenge to the church is that we too often stand with those who desire order first of all, rather than justice. Those with the power to impose order really have to bear the burden of injustice.

This challenge is well illustrated in two biblical events: the story of Solomon and his "great" achievements, and the story of Joseph.

In the biblical account of Solomon's reign there is a strand that speaks of his grand achievements and his great wisdom. Solomon seeks to bring royal order to the nation and royal control to the landscape—temple, city, bureaucracy, taxes, and the like. In reality he sought to end the tribal federation and regional power, developed a huge bureaucracy, had a standing army that did not depend on the people or God, and was fascinated with wisdom.[18] Yet it is, as 1 Kings 9 makes clear, an abusive, oppressive, and centralizing rule. In the end, the kingdom split because of the ruthlessness of his reign, and that of his son Rehoboam (1 Kgs 12:1–19).

The other story is of Joseph (Genesis 37–50),[19] which is, I suggest, a story about empire, although we who share such places of power rarely recognize it as such. Usually this has been told as a hero story in our children's church, so we lose its real edge. In brief, the story is that Joseph is sold by his jealous brothers into slavery (they may have had good reason for this jealousy, one must say), and he finishes up in Egypt. Joseph gains a good position, is betrayed by a woman scorned, and ends up in jail. Later he is called out of jail to interpret Pharoah's dream about famine and plenty and is put in charge of the famine preparation (Genesis 41). The rest of the story is about successful famine relief, eventual reunion with his family, and great prosperity in Egypt.

But notice a couple of things we often ignore. First, in Genesis 41:48, Joseph collected all the grain from the countryside, and stored it in the towns. He left the farmers without their grain, that which they would store in their community, and that they needed to replant, and he controlled the market from the city. Second, if you think this a bit far-fetched, consider Genesis 47:13–26: Joseph accumulated all the money in Egypt and Canaan, then all the livestock, and then all the land. Finally the people became serfs, sharecroppers on Pharoah's land. Empire cared not at all for the people through the famine, but only for the accumulation of power and wealth for the Pharoah and those at the centre. It is interesting that the priests kept their land. They had an allowance from Pharoah (Gen 47:22), because they served the purposes of the empire. Empire is about power at the centre and the removal of contested frontiers. There is to be no place of dispute or contention about life. Everything is to owe its life to the centre, to be dependent on the words of those at the middle of power—social, political, and religious.

The church's history has been marked by changes in the way it has related to those at this center—from opposition to support to sharing

18. Brueggemann, *The Prophetic Imagination*, 31.

19. The very important story of Tamar is inserted into the story at chapter 38, but I must leave that.

power to being the center to struggling to hold a place at the center. It is the struggle to determine whether "Jesus is Lord" is a counterclaim to empire or part of an affirmation about the way empire and church exercise the lordship of the absent Christ. It is about the way the church understands the relationship between order (for those at the center) and justice (for those on the fringes).

The church tradition since Augustine has largely reflected that emerging empire-related understanding of order and justice. Augustine, Luther, and Calvin were all concerned for justice, but each was convinced that the pursuit of justice should never endanger order and peace, and each believed that that order was a hierarchical one.[20] As Miguel De La Torre points out, this tradition is clearly reflected in modern scholarship. For example, James Gustafson says that liberative practice is all right as long as it doesn't upset society's equilibrium (which, of course, sustains the world of those with power and continues the marginalization of the poor). Paul Ramsey argued that the lunch sit-ins that protestors used to try to end segregation in the U.S.A. in the 1960s were improper because "they disrupted a well-ordered society"[21] and violated the right to private property. The existing well-ordered society was more crucial than the ending of racism. Yet the reality is that justice for the marginalized will always endanger the social order imposed by those who benefit from the impoverishment of members of the community. The whole point of such protest is to upset the order that oppresses it. The constant question for the church is where it sits in this debate as followers of the Christ who said we would find him among the imprisoned and marginalized (Matt 25:31–46).

The Nature of Justice

The second entry point into the theological landscape is the way in which we understand justice. There are a number of ways in which justice is understood and incorporated into the debate about order. For example, within our current judicial system there are two basic kinds of justice: retributive justice (including rehabilitative justice) and restor-

---

20. For a fuller explanation of these positions see De La Torre, *Doing Christian Ethics*, 27–30.

21. Ibid., 29.

ative justice.[22] While both are important to an understanding of justice, they are less crucial to this present discussion.

More important to our discussion are distributive and end-pattern justice. Distributive justice, which has its roots in liberal political philosophy and law, says that justice means that all people are treated the same. This is an important understanding of justice, particularly in the legal system, for it seeks to ensure that people are dealt with according to the merits of the case, regardless of their wealth, gender, ethnicity, or other factors. But in many areas of life this understanding of justice simply ignores the realities of power in our community. In many situations, treating everybody the same inevitably means that outcomes will always be unjust. What is promoted as common interests, as equality, are really the special interests of some, which are claimed as universal values. So, for example, if a particular community has been denied access to equal education, or if a culture exists in which a particular group defines the work situation, then equal treatment or equal access will mean that some do not get a fair go. "Positive discrimination" is based on this understanding of "end-pattern" justice. That is, a situation is not just simply because all people are treated the same, but because people have an equal opportunity to achieve the same results. This may mean that some people receive additional help to overcome historic and social factors that discriminate against them.

This sense of "end-pattern" justice is closely tied to what biblical commentator Ched Myers calls redistributive justice. This is a broad biblical concept of justice that is about shifting resources of power and wealth from the rich and powerful to the poor and oppressed in order to create a fair and equal society, the hallmarks of the kingdom of God. The process of redistributive justice in the biblical narrative also includes the dynamics of reconciliation, forgiveness, and reparation. They incorporate the principles of restorative justice.

As Myers has argued, redistributive justice must involve, for the rich, the act of repentance.[23] And there can be no repentance unless

22. Retributive justice assumes that justice is achieved when people are punished for their breach of the law (the crime being a crime against the state). A key characteristic of restorative justice is that it centers on the victim, and that a crime is a violation not simply of the law but of people and relationships. In order to achieve restorative justice, the offender is primarily accountable to the victim and then to the community.

23. Myers, *Who Will Roll Away the Stone?* 166.

there is reparation to the poor. In his analysis of the story of Jesus and the rich man (Mark 10:17–31), Myers claims that economic justice (which includes giving back to the poor) is a hallmark of the kingdom and of discipleship.[24] Fairness in resource distribution is also about equality in power. Luke eloquently states this in the Magnificat (Luke 1:46–55)—the revolutionary prescription of a transformed society under the reign of God announced by Mary upon the knowledge of her pregnancy: "He has shown strength with his arm; he has scattered the proud in the thoughts of their hearts. He has brought down the powerful from their thrones, and lifted up the lowly; he has filled the hungry with good things, and sent the rich away empty" (Luke 1:51–53). Power is redistributed (1:51–52), and at the same time so are resources (1:53). This is the nature of the kingdom of God.

The kingdom of God is about economics, because Jesus's kingdom is about another attempt to create the community of Israel as God desired that community to be after Egypt. This was a people of Jubilee, of redistribution of wealth, and of equality, a place for the stranger and orphan. This was a people who recognized that life, land, and themselves all belonged to God. Life is a gift and is to be lived that way. In this way of understanding the world—that was always challenged and undermined in Israel by those with power and wealth—everything is a gift, and our job is to make sure it circulates.

Second Peoples' Theology: Order and Justice

Justice, order, and accountability are important issues in a disordered world, and raise questions both about the presence of the life of the kingdom, and its sense of inclusive justice, and the providential care of God in a fallen world. How does a church, faced with abuse in Indigenous communities, and with the actions of governments to impose order, respond to these questions?

It seems to me that the first challenge is to the way the church locates itself within the received tradition that values order before justice. It is a tradition that is more concerned for the disorder and chaos that threatens those with power, than it is for the pursuit of justice as a sign of the presence of the kingdom for those who are the least. The church

24. Ibid., 161ff.

has sought in recent years to break open that tradition but still too easily seeks order rather than putting justice at its absolute heart.

This means that theological conversation in Australia needs to occur alongside people, and not simply from a distance, being aware of the diversity of voices that arise in the Indigenous community, and being aware of those who are doubly oppressed—women and children. It is to continually ask ourselves who we are listening to, and why we have privileged those voices. It is to be self-critical, aware of the danger that our response is shaped by ideology rather than the real situation, but also aware of the temptation to short-term and pragmatic responses, rather than to the long-term task of social transformation and empowerment. It is to raise critical questions about the assumption of modernity that each human being is completely free and accountable for all that they do, or that they are so shaped by circumstances, that they are not accountable.

We assume that freedom—by which we mean freedom from the restrictions placed on us by others—and personal moral responsibility are part of the very structure of human life. But the Christian faith claims that what makes us human is not that we are free to construct our own life and meaning. We are people made in the image of God, a God who is Trinitarian. It is also the claim of the church that humanity is fallen in the sense that as a whole it is separated from God, who is the source of its life. While there has often been an attempt to make what we know as sin into a moral category that connects to the language of blame, it is actually a relational category that touches our place in social and historical life.

The argument in chapter 3 about our encounter with God in the life of the marginalized other also implies that sin is the refusal of that encounter. This means that abuse and other unjust events are not simply actions but distorted and damaged relationships. People do not simply have a will that is unencumbered and autonomous. Our will to do things, our determination to act in certain ways, is inescapable from all the events and relationships that form us as persons. So, as Alistair McFadyen says, the relationship between human freedom and culpability is more complex than things like the intervention suggest. At one level, people are free to make decisions and are culpable. There is self-orientation, self-direction, and human willing, but it is a willing that is subject to profound disorientation.[25] There is a wider societal culpability that needs to be brought to expression so that we can also speak of God's creating and saving action.

This means we need to develop a theology of accountability that cannot consist of accusations of culpability thrown from afar. It is not that people are not responsible, but it is a distorted responsibility that can only be dealt with inside relationships that bring people back into the presence of God and offer healing. It is a healing that draws on Christian insights about excommunication, not as a casting out and exclusion, but as a removal from community to allow for protection of survivors and time for change. That is, within a Christian theology, the outcome is not punishment; neither is it lack of accountability because of circumstances. The aim is genuine relationships worked out in the context of a humanity immersed in circumstances often beyond their control. It is the possibility that through a reorientation to God, people will find their disordered willing pulled by the Holy Spirit towards new and genuine relationships with others and with God. Jesus opposes sin, not by condemnation, but "by energising a counter-dynamic that reorients people in their relationships one with another and with God (love of God and neighbor as oneself)."[26]

But, as has been suggested already, this does not mean a theology for dealing with disorder that either punishes from a distance or allows people to escape because of mitigating circumstances. Within the disorder of human life, there is a need for structures of order and accountability. The mistake of the intervention was that by imposing order and a solution to abuse, it further undermined any chance of restoring structures of order within communities. The significant issue in this theology of order and the providence of God is that the goal of order is not the order of the center or the empire. It is the order of the kingdom or reign of God. It is the needed order of the people on the margins, an order necessary not for control but for human life. It is order for the good of the people, not for protection of power and social order that serves the needs of those with power. It is order whose heart is justice, and which may disturb colonial and imperial order for justice to emerge.

25. McFadyen, *Bound to Sin*, 147.
26. Ibid., 223.

The intervention assumed that justice meant treating everyone the same and integrating them into a consumerist economy. The church must face the more difficult challenge of its role in creating space through its own actions for redistributive justice, for real sharing of wealth with those most disadvantaged.

One of the dangers of liberal theology and the turn to the self is that there is no place to deal seriously with sin and evil. People are seen as generally good, and bad behavior is caused by outside forces like the structures of society or, in psychological theories, family history and patterns of earlier relationships. Interestingly enough, a community obsessed with freedom makes people captive to the fate of our families or other relationships, denying any responsibility to people for how they respond to their life's circumstances. How does the church speak of the absolute reality of evil in the light of abuse, intervention, and lack of government funding for Indigenous communities?

Racism is always an underlying subtext in the public struggles in Australia; a racism marked by paternalism, control, and political advantage, abuse of power (including funding), and the desire both to hide people and to shame them. In the New Testament story of the healing of the woman who had been bleeding for twelve years (Mark 5:24b–34), a story about public shame and honor, we gain two insights in terms of our task. First, for whatever reason, it was a shameful thing for this woman to be in public, and more so as she deliberately touched Jesus. In addressing her as "daughter" (5:34), Jesus establishes a relationship in which the touch is acceptable, and allows her to be in this public space. Second, in this society shaped by honor and shame, it would have been expected for Jesus to claim credit for her healing, thus claiming honor and making her dependent. Instead he said, "your faith has made you whole," allowing her to be responsible for her own healing, and thus to gain respect and honor.

The act of theology in this country in the face of injustice needs to be an act of shaping practices that enable an invisible people to be in a public place without shame. It is an act of naming people as children of God and providing the space for them to be welcomed in the public place. It is a building and honoring of relationships that deny invisibility.

How does the church learn to listen to voices it has often ignored, particularly the voices of women; not middle-class and articulate women but women on the margins? The temptation of the church that is still significantly patriarchal in structure and ethos is that it privileges the voice of men without thought, and assumes that a male-headed hierarchy is normal. In discussing Asian feminist theology and the impact of the same colonial powers that were involved in Australia, Pui-Lan Kwok speaks of the way women have been portrayed in their own culture and by colonial powers. The colonial powers stereotyped women in ways that made them compliant to the colonial agenda and promoted the domination of men over women. While women played a significant role in the struggle for independence, this role has "been downplayed by both male elites and historians, for whom regaining political autonomy meant not so much the liberation of people as a whole, but rather the overthrow of foreign masters and the redeeming of 'Asian manhood.'"[27] This denial of the place of women in post-colonial society has been supported by myths about pure Asian culture, and what it means to be a real Asian woman. This position is often mirrored in Indigenous society, where there are myths about the place of women in traditional society. The church needs to find a way to honor the voice of women, and to respectfully question the way men seek to be the only voice that can tell the story of where women fit in society (or to determine which women can speak).

Conclusion

The theological challenge is how the church moves to real solutions and not just vague generalizations and policies, and how those practical things actually relate to the theological claims. What is clear, if the church is an expression of God's providential care and a sign of the coming kingdom, is that it cannot do this theology apart from real engagement with Indigenous people. Theology in this case is about practices based in long-term solidarity, in its own commitment to redistributive justice, in speaking that does not shame people, and in imagining with Indigenous people what options there are beside what seem to be pragmatically inevitable.

Political pragmatism tends to deal with the symptoms and to be judged in terms of short-term goals. Evil is for a time contained, or removed in its present form. And this may be necessary, but it does not

27. Kwok, *Introducing Asian Feminist Theology*, 17.

take away the long-term need. And the danger is that the pragmatic approach may itself cause unforeseen stresses on the social lives of those that it touches. The alternative position is to see that the history we are faced with is often defined by those with power to define it, and is not simply a given (i.e., there is no independently real world on which we act); and the situation is not final, for it needs to be seen within the end purposes of God. The God of Jesus Christ is concerned not just to contain evil, but to root out the very source of that evil.

The intervention did not help people take responsibility for or control of their own lives. It reinforced power at the center. It misunderstood justice, and it defined people within the restrictions of a consumerist culture. The church needs to continue its critique, with and alongside Indigenous peoples.

6

The Practice of Being Church

ECCLESIOLOGY—OUR THEOLOGY OF THE CHURCH—IS A STATEMENT about where Christians are in the world, who they sit with, and what they affirm and challenge. In this chapter the question is, what are the essential signs or marks of the church in this place as we confront our history and the present relationships between Indigenous and Second peoples?

Stories that Speak of the Church

In August 1982 a group of Indigenous leaders met at Crystal Creek in Queensland as part of a Christian Conference of Asia Urban Rural Mission Consultation, and began to talk about their own Indigenous church. A national conference was held at Galiwin'ku in August 1983, bringing together Indigenous Christians to speak about their place in the Uniting Church in Australia (UCA). The national assembly of the UCA agreed to recognize the Uniting Aboriginal and Islander Christian Congress (UAICC) in 1985, handing it the responsibility to lead ministry to and with Indigenous people.[1] In 1988 the assembly established a covenant between the UAICC and other parts of the Uniting Church that expressed a commitment to mutual ministry and to sharing of resources and control of ministry. However grand the assembly's intention, the experience of UAICC has been that the structures and actions of the church have not given them appropriate control of ministry, access to resources, or a proper voice in the councils of the church.

---

1. For an account of the factors that led to the establishment of the UAICC, see William W. Emilsen, "The Origins of the Uniting Aboriginal and Islander Christian Congress," in Emilsen and Emilsen, *Mapping the Landscape.*

For example, at the 2003 assembly the issue of sexuality and leadership dominated the agenda. The UAICC was adamant that the issue the church was being asked to decide—that gay and lesbian people could be admitted to ordained ministry—was contrary to their theology, and to traditional culture. They asked the church to respect their position, and the covenant relationship that exists within the UC, and not proceed with the decision. The challenge in that conversation was, how does one become part of the church, and what are the obligations and rights that come with membership? To what extent are these things established by the tradition, and to what extent does meaning arise in a conversation and relationship? Were these things settled by the dominant reading of the tradition, and could any conversation only be about helping people see what these meant?

I made a speech in which I argued that the basis for decisions about ministry and sexuality were first of all issues about baptism. Baptism was the founding and primary covenant that allowed people to be called to ministry—at least I believed that to be the Reformed position. Baptism is the prior covenant, and other covenants need to be sorted out in the context of that claim. Over lunch that day, my Indigenous friends rebuked me severely and said I needed to spend time with some of them discovering the nature of covenant. I still feel and remember the enormous pain of that rebuke, and my frustration at trying to explain and defend how I understood the relationship between context and tradition. What I missed in the initial part of that conversation was that my friends were challenging the way I did theology. I had assumed that I could understand what the signs of the church (like baptism) meant before I entered into a relationship and conversation. I had assumed that the matter was settled by tradition, understood from within my context. I didn't actually enter or foster a dialogue between tradition and context but imposed the tradition onto the context.

Here is a second story. Three non-Indigenous ministers laid a complaint against another non-Indigenous minister who was working for the UAICC, the charge being disrespect for the councils of the church and for colleagues in ministry. The UAICC claimed the right to deal with this matter, while the complainants' synod claimed that the matter belonged to it because the minister in question was under its oversight. The UAICC asked for a presidential ruling on whose responsibility it was under the constitution and regulations of the Uniting Church, and in the light of the covenant between the UCA and UAICC. The president ruled that the regulations gave the authority to the synod.

What was clear in the discussion around the ruling was that the covenant had no impact on a reading of the constitution and regulations. For some UAICC leaders, this was a most difficult interpretation, for they had hoped that the request for a ruling would have allowed conversation, and respect for the covenant relationship, not simply a legalistic reading. They believed that relationships were more crucial than the rules.[2]

The issue raised by these two stories is an issue of ecclesiology, of the nature of the church, and how we know that it actually is the church. What were also at stake in the situations of both stories were the assumptions that shape discourse within the church around Indigenous members. I believe that most non-Aboriginal people involved in the discussion implicitly believed that the nature of the church was settled, and that the covenant might change minor things but could never touch on the essential nature of the church. Covenant was about where people fitted within the church, rather than what sort of church the UCA wished to be. There was, I believe, an inability to hear, because while people thought that they were speaking a common language of covenant, the framing discourse was different. As has been suggested in the analysis of racism, non-Aboriginal Australians exist within racial discourse without much awareness that they do so. So, while church people approach this sort of conversation with great goodwill, and while they may be committed to a covenant relationship, often they inadvertently still see covenant through a tacitly racist framework.

The challenge from UAICC, it seems to me, is: Can the church be the church in Australia if it does not properly honor the place of the Indigenous people in its life? That honoring is not just finding a place for people in what is already set and decided, but allowing people's voices to really be heard in ways that challenge how people understand the marks of the church. It asks whether a necessary mark

2. There is evidence that the UAICC sought a ruling despite clear advice that the president would rule against their claim, in order to make the church's position on covenant and on responsibility for ministry really clear. They wanted to know exactly where they stood in the midst of all the fine words. Some people were quite upset about this strategy. What needs to be remembered, though, is that the rules governing efforts by minority people to seek their own liberation may need to be different from rules governing those who exercise control.

of the church must be the presence of those who are the First peoples, as genuine partners in the church—as people who are the church and not just objects of the church. It suggests that relationships are crucial to what it means to be church.

The Tradition or Theological Landscape

One of the reasons for exploring the tradition is to remind ourselves that the present situation is not the only way we can understand the church. It is also to help us reclaim some of the minor parts of our tradition, what Douglas John Hall calls, in another context, "thin tradition."[3]

The ecclesiological landscape is very broad, certainly beyond the scope of this chapter.[4] I have sought to enter the landscape at those points that seemed most relevant to the issues being raised within the context: what is the church; what do we mean by "One, Holy, Catholic, and Apostolic"; and what images and models of the church are most helpful?

What Is the Church?

Miroslav Volf develops an understanding of the church that is found in Jesus's words in Matthew: "For where two or three are gathered in my name, I am there among them" (18:20). He suggests that since Ignatius of Antioch, the understanding of the church is that the church is wherever Jesus Christ or the Spirit (really the Spirit of Christ) is. This is not to suggest that the church alone has the Spirit, but that the church is present where the Spirit of Christ "is present in its *ecclesially constitutive* activity."[5] Through the participation of the Spirit of Christ in the church, there is a mutual indwelling of the triune God and the people of

---

3. Hall, *The Cross in Our Context*, 13. He was talking about the theology of the cross as a thin tradition.

4. This exploration leaves aside a number of significant questions in ecclesiology: ministry, episcope (oversight), polity (the structures of the church), election, authority and hierarchy, sacraments, the meaning of the "local" church, and conciliarity and primacy, for example. For those who want to explore issues further a good beginning point is Migliore, *Faith Seeking Understanding* (chapter 11), Kärkkäinen, *An Introduction to Ecclesiology*; Moltmann, *The Church in the Power of the Spirit*; World Council of Churches, *The Nature and Purpose of the Church*; Watson, *Introducing Feminist Ecclesiology*.

5. Volf, *After Our Likeness*, 129 (italics original).

the church, which is not simply an object of hope for the eschatological future but is a present experience.[6]

Given the ecumenical consensus that the church is the church because of the presence of the Spirit of Christ, a central issue is how this Spirit comes to or is mediated to the church. What gathering of people constitutes the church as church? Contrary to those traditions which insist that the presence of Christ is mediated to the local church by the universal church (thorough, for example, sacraments, bishops, or hierarchy), Volf says that the presence of Christ comes directly to the people of God as a congregation. The church is properly an assembly of people who gather in the name of Christ, which means that they identify with him and attest that he is the one who determines their lives. This is a people who socially and publicly profess faith in Jesus Christ, and commit themselves to a certain way of life that depends on that belief in Christ. This confession is never just private and individual but always occurs before others and has a social, public and political dimension.[7] The church does not cease to be church when it is not assembled but continues through the mutual care of the people for one another and through commitment to mission.

Because the church is born through the presence of the Spirit of Christ, it is necessarily charismatic. Volf says there are five features of this charismatic church.[8]

- The exalted Christ himself is acting in the gifts of the Spirit.

- The gifts of the Spirit are universally distributed among all the people and are not restricted to some particular group, which implies a common responsibility for, and mutual subordination in, the church's life.

- No person has all the gifts, but their fullness is found in the whole community, so that there is a mutual interdependence in the church.

- The bestowal of gifts is a free act of the Spirit, not a demand of the church.

6. Ibid., 128–29.
7. Ibid., 145–49.
8. Ibid., 228–33.

- Spiritual gifts can vary at different times and in different circumstances, with gifts coming to the fore as important for the community or moving into the background as unimportant for the
  community at that time.

"In summary, the ecclesiality of the church can be defined as follows: *Every congregation that assembles around the one Jesus Christ as Savior and Lord in order to profess faith in him publicly in pluriform fashion, including through baptism an-d the Lord's Supper, and which is open to all churches of God and to all human beings, is a church in the full sense of the word, since Christ promised to be present in it through his Spirit as the first fruits of the gathering of the whole people of God in the eschatological reign of God.*"[9]

One, Holy, Catholic, and Apostolic

The central question faced by the church is, how do we know that a particular community actually is the church? It is a question that usually arises in time of crisis. One such example was the Donatist crisis of the fourth century, when some people claimed to be the pure and real church because they had been faithful through persecution while others had not. (This controversy was eventually resolved by the claim that church is both saints and sinners). Another crisis was the struggle at the time of the Reformation for the Reformers to prove that they were still the real church though separated from Rome (often this discussion involved an argument about how the apostolic character of the church was guaranteed). The most central tradition of the church says that the true church is one, holy, catholic, and apostolic; that is, that there is unity, holiness, universality, and a faith that is aligned with the apostles.

The World Council of Churches' document *The Nature and Purpose of the Church* provides a good summary of what this means in the church.

> Being the creature of God's own Word and Spirit the Church
> of God is one, holy, catholic and apostolic. These essential attri-
> butes of the Church are not its own qualities but are fully rooted
> in its dependence upon God through his Word and Spirit. It is
> one because the God who binds it to himself by Word and Spirit
> is the one creator and redeemer making the Church a foretaste

9. Ibid., 158 (italics original).

and instrument of the redemption of all created reality. It is holy because God is the holy one who in Jesus Christ has overcome all unholiness, sanctifying the Church by his word of forgiveness in the Holy Spirit and making it his own, the body of Christ. It is catholic because God is the fullness of life who through Word and Spirit makes the church the place and instrument of his saving, life-giving, fulfilling presence wherever it is, thereby offering the fullness of the revealed Word, all the means of salvation to people of every nation, race, class, sex and culture. It is apostolic because the Word of God that creates and sustains the Church is the Gospel primarily and normatively borne witness to by the apostles, making the communion of the faithful a community that lives in, and is responsible for, the succession of the apostolic truth through the ages.[10]

The ecclesiologies of the various churches are particular expressions of the concern that they be one, holy, catholic, and apostolic. For example, in *On the Councils and the Church* (1539), Martin Luther suggests that there were seven distinguishing marks of the church: possessing the Scriptures; and preaching, hearing, believing, confessing, and acting the word of God; the sacraments of baptism and the altar; the ministry and the office of loosing and binding; proper public worship; and bearing the cross.[11]

John Calvin says that there are two essential features of the Church—the Word of God preached and heard, and proper administration of the sacraments—and there can be a degree of failure or diversity on other matters as long as these are present.[12]

One of the tensions in the tradition is the disagreement around sanctification and holiness, and whether the church can be holy in this still-sinful world. We see this tension in the Methodist insistence that holiness is a mark of the church, and in the Calvinist position that while holiness is important, it cannot be an essential mark. The importance of this issue of holiness is whether the present church, this broken and imperfect community, is really the church. Can this group of people who

10. World Council of Churches, *The Nature and Purpose of the Church*; Report of the Joint Commission between the Roman Catholic Church and World Methodist Council, *The Apostolic Tradition* (1986–1991, Fifth Series) is a helpful introduction to the issue of apostolic faith.

11. McGrath, *The Christian Theology Reader*, has an extract from Luther that is concerned for the central mark of the word of God (475–77).

12. Calvin, *Institutes*, bk 4, chap 1, para. 9–10.

are still sinful and who, in our world, may be made up of believers and unbelievers really show the signs of the church? Can it actually embody those practices that are the church?

These issues of holiness and the visibility of the church really arise because the church is not made up entirely of believers. Because of the time the church has spent at the heart of Christendom, and the expectation that citizenship and church membership were coextensive, there are questions about whether the visible church is the real church, or whether the real church is necessarily invisible. Volf, for example, insists that there is a sociality to salvation, because it brings one into communion with both God and other people. To believe is to bring one into communion with God (who is three "persons"), and with everyone else who has entrusted themselves to the God revealed in Jesus Christ. This cannot simply be communion within the invisible church, because one comes to faith only within the concrete social form of the church where Christ is present.

Volf's position on visibility reflects his free-church tradition's affirmation of a believers' church, which is a voluntary and consciously joined community that places emphasis on separation from the world and calls all members to witness and service. Those who hold to a believers' church are seeking a Christian community which is an "assembly of the righteous" rather than a mixed body. They seek the gathering of those who have been truly converted, have been regenerated by the Holy Spirit, and are radically obedient to God.

One other important mark of the church for those in the Reformed tradition is the ministry of the whole people of God, founded in the idea of the priesthood of all believers—the idea that all baptized people share in the priestly and kingly office of Jesus (1 Pet 2:9). This leads to the view that each Christian person has a responsibility to bear the burden of others and to share responsibility for the life of the church, and also has a right to preach the Word and to administer absolution and discipline.[13]

Biblical Images

The way the world is socially structured and defended relies on language, symbol, image, and myth. Images, like other forms of communication,

13. Kärkkäinen, *Introduction to Ecclesiology*, 42–43.

shape what we know and how we describe the world. They structure relationships between people, as we see illustrated in the cartoons and other images that mark racist discourse. Images are shaped by particular contexts and are always culturally and historically relative. In the church, the images we use are usually shaped by denominational history, geography, social class, institutional considerations, historical circumstances, and social location. They are chosen to support and defend certain interests. The images we have for *church* in the New Testament both enable us to see what church is and limit how we understand.

There are a variety of images of church, and no image is intended to be exclusive but to point to other dimensions and images.[14] Among the important images are

- The church as the people of God, which points to covenant and pilgrimage.

- The church as a servant people, which is based on Jesus's claim that he has come as a servant (e.g. Mark 10:45). The church is to enter into costly service (Matt 20:25–26).

- The church as the body of Christ (Rom 12:5; 1 Cor 12:12; Eph 1:23), which is entered by baptism, and where all members are given gifts for the building up of the body (Rom 12:4–8; 1 Cor 12:4–30).

- The church as the temple of the Holy Spirit, a place where the Spirit dwells and is able to provide life from within.

These images reflect the Trinitarian dimensions of the church. There are others that pick up other aspects of faith and community: vine (interrelationship and dependence on Christ), flock (trust and obedience), wedding party (the eschatological reality of the church), and bride (the intimate, subordinate relationship of the church to Christ). Pui-Lan Kwok, on the other hand, talks of the church in terms of images of the people of God (referring to a chosen people), the body of Christ (more about corporate life, plurality of gifts, and dignity of all), and the model of the "Jesus community." This community was formed when

14. There are three particularly helpful references in regard to images: World Council of Churches, *The Nature and Purpose of the Church*; Migliore, *Faith Seeking Understanding*; and Minear, *Images of the Church*. Minear lists ninety-six images or analogies of the church in the New Testament.

Jesus proclaimed the good news of the new creation, which is found in the kingdom. "The 'Jesus community' was a visible and dynamic sign of the kingdom oriented toward a radical transformation of the political and religious establishment of the time."[15] They all need to be held together to give a complete understanding of the church and its place in the purpose of God.

Models

In addition to biblical images of the church, there have traditionally been a number of theological models of the church. They tend to include similar features but give a different emphasis to various aspects. Daniel Migliore suggests that there are currently five models of the church: an institution of salvation, an elite community of the Holy Spirit, a sacrament of salvation, a herald of the good news, and a servant of the servant Lord. He suggests that we may need a new model in which the church is new life in communion with the dancing, communal, Trinitarian God.[16] That is, the church is a sign and provisional realization of the destiny of humanity and the whole creation—participation in and reflection of the triune love of God.

Veli-Matti Kärkkäinen suggests an alternative way of seeing the models:

- The Orthodox sense of the church as an icon of the Trinity, a community that seeks to represent, and be an image of the unity in diversity, which is a mark of God.

- The Roman Catholic sense of the church as the people of God, a pilgrim people on the way to God's intended end.

- Martin Luther's emphasis on the noninstitutional character of the church as a gathering of believers who are the church because of the Word of God and true faith.

- Karl Barth's understanding that the church is primarily a witnessing and called community, and one in which the gifts of the Spirit are affirmed for all people.

---

15. Kwok, *Introducing Asian Feminist Theology*, 110.

16. Migliore, *Faith Seeking Understanding*, 255–65.

- The free-church claim that the church is a fellowship of believers, in which ordinary people have a responsibility to interpret and live out the Scriptures, and in which they have direct access to God.

- The Pentecostal emphasis on the church as a community that exists in the power of the Spirit, which is the mark of the presence of God.[17]

An issue being raised in this chapter is whether the available images and models are helpful or of limited use in describing the church in Australia and its relationship with Indigenous peoples.

Some Questions of the Tradition

While I do not share Vatican II's understanding of the church as a sacrament,[18] I do believe that the church is to be a sign of God's presence and desire for the world. Therefore, the church has patterns of actions and meanings that find expression in such symbols as prayer, worship, and sacraments. These symbolic actions of the church are meant, as Nicholas Lash says, to be "legible."[19] That is, all of humanity is meant to see in the church a sign of God's saving presence and the unity (and diversity) intended for all humankind.

The church can fail in its vocation in two ways. First, it can fail because what it does, where it locates itself, and who it relates to contradict what the church says about itself. It ceases to be "legible." Second, it fails when the symbols that are used "are (by and large) expressive only of the history and experience of some one class or interest-group, some one race, culture, sex or nation."[20] In this case, the church is an impoverished sign of the unity and diversity of humankind that is to be found in the mysterious life of the Trinitarian God.

Feminist scholar Natalie Watson reminds us that for many women this is precisely what the church is: an impoverished sign that does

---

17. Kärkkäinen, *Introduction to Ecclesiology*.

18. *The Dogmatic Constitution of the Church* (*Lumen Gentium*) says that the church is called to be the sacrament of humanity's union with God and of unity for the whole human race. (art. 1). See Flannery, *The Conciliar and Post-Conciliar Documents*, 350.

19. Lash, *Theology on the Way to Emmaus*, 24.

20. Ibid., 24–25.

not take seriously the experience of women in the life of the church.[21] Implicit in her work is a critique not just of patriarchy but also of racism, and of the exclusion of people on the basis of color and race.

Her first issue is the way we talk about women and their relationship with the church, using language like "women and the church," or "the churches in solidarity with women." The implication of this language is that women are an issue to be dealt with by the church, when in fact women are the church. There are not two realities (women and church), but a church that is constituted by women and men.[22]

Watson's second issue is the way the church is described as vital religious space, but then that such a description is used to support "a particular, predominantly patriarchal social symbolic order."[23] That is, the church precludes women from a full place in that space.

Third for Watson, the central question is not, what is the church? which leads to an institutional response, but, who is the church? which leads to a communal response. The issue is, who makes up the church, and who is allowed to flourish within that community?[24]

Fourth, Watson questions some of the models of church (the bride of Christ, the body of Christ, the servant) on the grounds that they are based on patriarchal assumptions about women and their submission to men, that they allow only men to represent the male Christ, and that the models assume that women are usually subservient and helpful to others and are encouraged to suffer. Rather, Watson says, they need to be more affirming of their women's value and of the claim that women too bear God's image. What is needed is not a church "for" others (Bonhoeffer), but a church "with" others.

Fifth, she questions the way the church has understood the terms *one, holy, catholic,* and *apostolic.* Unity is often made to mean sameness, and the exclusion of diversity; and this means all people must become like those with most power. Holiness is defined in ways that exclude some (e.g., women) or is used as an exclusive claim that suggests no one else is holy. Catholicity is sometimes claimed as if the church already fully embodied the future eschatological hope. Apostolicity is some-

---

21. Watson, *Introducing Feminist Ecclesiology.*

22. Ibid., 1.

23. Ibid., 6.

24. Ibid., 9, 118–19.

times used to exclude women (in ministry, as not being in the line of male apostles), when it can be seen as the whole church's continuing the vision of the early church for equality and justice.[25]

As well as raising questions about the traditional way the church has described itself, Watson suggests some ways of thinking about the church that are helpful for this chapter. Drawing on Orthodox ecclesiology, she suggests that we see the church less as an institution and more as a mode of being, a way of existence. The church is meant to express a radical openness to the continuing story of God in the world, particularly as that story is told by those whose voice is often not heard. The church needs to be a place where those who are excluded "can hear each other into speech."[26] The church needs to be a place where all people "begin to find spaces in which they can flourish and enable each other to flourish and live in relationships of justice."[27] The foundation for this sort of community is the Trinitarian God, whose relationship to the world encourages human flourishing.

In Nicholas Lash's and Natalie Watson's analysis we have the fundamental challenge to ecclesiology in Australia as that was illustrated in our opening stories. The church does not express in its life a sense of the equality, unity, and diversity of all humankind, particularly in regard to Indigenous people. Whatever the good intentions of the church, it shares the discourse of racism in this country, which shapes even the language of covenant and reconciliation. And it is churches whose shaping symbols, and sense of what the church is, have been determined within other cultures and other times: particular and contextual symbols declared to be universal.

What Do We Say about Ecclesiology in Australia?

The theological landscape in regard to the church provides a set of models and images that seek to give us an idea of what the church could look like. It seeks to provide an understanding of when a community truly is the church, and not some other body of people. The stories that began this chapter ask a number of questions of that landscape. Whose voice and experience is to be taken most seriously? Does the voice of

25. Ibid., 111–13.
26. Ibid., 116.
27. Ibid., 118.

Indigenous people have a particularly privileged place in the conversation? What does the symbolic action of baptism say about the unity and diversity of the church? Is the life and structure of the church settled apart from a relationship with Indigenous people?

Churches and theologians describe the marks of the church to defend certain personal and institutional interests. For example, unity can be defined in a way that excludes diversity, and to reinforce the sort of sameness and order desired by those in power. This means that the oneness of the church will always revolve around those qualities determined by those who have most influence in the church.

I wish to argue that the continuity or identity of the church is not found in common beliefs, structures, liturgy, or ministry but in the habits of life and associations shared by its members. It is not our sameness that holds us together, but the way people negotiate through their multiple relationships and ways of being, and their common theological location—i.e. their commitment to be where Christ is with the least in the world. Beginning with a commitment to diversity in the church, Yung Suk Kim, for example, explores the way that the "body of Christ" metaphor in 1 Corinthians 12:27 is less about church, boundaries, and unity, than it is a metaphor for "living out Christ" or for Christ's work.[28] His argument is that the body of Christ is the body of the crucified one, and that we are "in Christ" as we live his marginalized, crucified life (which "deconstructs society's wisdom, power and glory."[29]) Unity in Christ does not depend on being part of the same ecclesial body "but rather is a matter of having a mind and purpose framed by the same gospel that does not empty the cross of Christ of its power."[30] The body of Christ is more than the Christian community, but the community is an agent of the embodiment of Christ. Thus the argument Paul has is always with those who claim that their way of eating, their speaking in tongues, or their other activities are the *only* way to be in Christ.

So, whatever the oneness of the church means in Australia, it means that the church is a community that includes diverse people who are committed to serve the crucified and suffering one in various ways. Unity means forging a community that has the ability to hear alterna-

28. Kim, *Christ's Body in Corinth*, 94.

29. Ibid., 53.

30. Ibid., 74.

tive voices and is less interested in defining the boundaries that exclude than it is in remaining open to new voices, new claims, competing assertions and ways of seeing the world. It is a unity that is constantly forged in relationship with others.

The struggle for identity and recognition is often the source of human conflict as one human being or group refuses to recognize the other and their full humanity. Yet as James Perkinson suggests, the great danger is often that recognition may occur without conflict, that one group of people may unilaterally confer freedom on the other.[31] One group may unmake oppression, slavery, or unfreedom from their side only. There is actually no reciprocity of recognition. That which is given, is given on the terms of the one who has control. It makes no change in the life of the oppressed, and may be taken away at any time. Indeed, it is an upheaval in one community that changes neither; nor does it actually alter the relationship of power between them. Identity emerges not in genuine struggle, and a conversation that changes the identity of both, but in *in*difference and paternalism.[32]

It seems to me that this is the danger that accompanied the establishment of the UAICC within the church, and also of the covenant relationship that exists within the Uniting Church. While asked for by Indigenous people, the covenant was granted without real struggle. It didn't change the church but was a way of controlling change or of managing the challenge that the UAICC posed to the nature of the church and its self-understanding. It was act of well-meaning people that runs the risk of simply covering up difference with an image of unity, and when people challenge this, they are said to be disrupting the well-being of the church.

This understanding of unity in the church suggests that difficult conversations do not end with one side giving way. The conversations need to remain open, and to be deliberately held open, and not closed off, or the differences pushed underground for the sake of a false unity. This is what UAICC sought to do by asking the church not to decide about sexuality and ministry.[33] What was being asked in the request for a

31. Perkinson, *White Theology*, 75–78. He is drawing on the work of Frantz Fanon, *Black Skin, White Masks*.

32. Perkinson, *White Theology*, 77.

33. At the same time, it must be recognized that there are times of struggle about inclusion and justice where not deciding is to keep unity at the price of justice, is to

presidential ruling was, is the issue of who has responsibility for ministry closed by a simple ruling; is our life dictated by one reading of the rules; do the needs of white people take a priority over the needs of Indigenous people; or is what shapes us the nature of our relationships? Is it all sorted out so that we have to fit in, or is there space for more talk?

At the Melbourne Assembly in 2003, the UAICC asked another crucial question: does our life as Indigenous people, as the First peoples of the land, have a privileged place in the church? There are two very difficult issues in this for the church.

The first issue arises from the claim that the discussion about gay and lesbian people was contrary to Indigenous theology (their way of being Christian) and culture (their identity as Indigenous people). The issue is, can we non-Aboriginal people ever question that claim, or must we only accept the claim and work out our response? Can we ever suggest that what we are hearing is one voice in what has been a diverse culture, or is such a claim just another form of colonial determining of who speaks, and who is to be heard?

Mudrooroo says that "his mob," what he calls "Us Mob," were never a single mob. "We were many, as many as the trees, as the different types of animals."[34] The idea of a single Indigenous or Aboriginal people is the construct of colonizers, for in reality identity rests in regions (often inscribed on maps by white people to order the world). Nor was the culture unchanging, a claim that wants to make real Indigenous people a stone-age relic—an effort to name and control the other. Women, who had a significant place among "Us Mob," were redefined by the Master script as only able to be seen through and in relation to males (the European, patriarchal system). Being Indigenous is not simply about blood (for that is the Master's game), but is also learned; essentially it is about relationships and kinship, and how that orders the world. There are those, Mudrooroo says, who seek to see Us Mobs as one and to implement the Master's plans and policies. Mostly, though, those who have colonized have imposed patriarchy and hierarchy, and some have accepted this and now claim it was the way things have always been.[35]

---

keep order at the cost of new life for the marginalized. I think there was some danger of that in the sexuality debate, where supporting the UAICC's position would have made life harder for gay and lesbian people.

34. Mudrooroo, *Us Mob*, vi.

35. Ibid., 26–27.

The question remains open. How does the church ensure that it hears all voices and does not simply privilege one voice and one position? On what basis can Second peoples make comment or offer criticism when Indigenous peoples make assertions that are based in claims about their culture and speak against equality for women, for example, or insist on hierarchy rather than equal community?

The second issue is, among those resources and voices that enable us to encounter God, to be the church as a people where Christ is, what place is there for an Indigenous voice? The UAICC claims that their voice should be heard because they are First peoples, a people put here by God, and this has something to teach the church about being church. I think that being First peoples does give people a primary right to be heard that grows out of their relationship within the church. And as a people who have been made "other" in society and church, they are a community where we can encounter Christ. It is this voice the church must hear—an Indigenous voice that has been shoved to the margins.

What happens to baptism and my claim about the covenantal, renewing act and its place in determining the life of the church? I think it is right that baptism is the core symbolic act of the church, a sign of election and grace, and a claim that membership cannot be overturned by other claims. To overturn the claim of baptism would be to open ourselves to what the church has too often been guilty of: segregated churches; divisions between the baptized because of race, gender, class, or nation. Where I was wrong in my defense of a meaning of baptism, though, was to believe that I and the church (in its tradition) knew already what relationships are implied in baptism before I had explored that with Indigenous people. I thought such meanings were clear and pre-established, that others had to fit into what was actually a white, male, European view of baptism, a universal view that took too little account of the local and contextual implications of baptism and its meaning for concrete forms of discipleship.

The answer to the question, how do we know that this community in Australia is the church? is inseparable from the question of where we encounter Christ. That is, issues of unity, holiness, catholicity, and carrying the apostolic witness can only be understood relationally, and in particular, as involving a just relationship with Indigenous peoples. For example, however we understand the holiness of the church, it must involve a relationship with Indigenous people that is just, inclusive, and equal.

This does not mean that our actions determine whether or not we are the church. The church is church because of the presence of Christ, and the belief (made possible by the Spirit) of people. As Miroslav Volf says, the church does not cease to be the church because of lack of fruits of the Spirit, but Christ and the fruits are absent when people confess with their lips rather than their hearts.[36] The Reformed tradition says the church is where the word is rightly proclaimed and heard, and where the sacraments celebrated. My argument is that the word is not rightly proclaimed and heard just because it appears to accord to the biblical text or gets a verbal amen from the people, but because it expresses God's vision for equality and justice and locates God's people along with those on the margins. The church is both doxological and political—i.e., it is a real body engaged with the world and a community whose heart is praise of God.

I think Volf is right when he says that the church is where people confess Christ consciously. Christ is among the poor and the oppressed, but that does not make them church, or unconscious Christians. Those among whom we move do not tell us what the church is, but only where it must be if we wish to be with Christ. My question, though, is whether this distinction (between *what* and *where*) is as clear as it seems. Can we distinguish this easily between who we are, and where we are to be located? If a people remind us of where we will encounter Christ, have they not also told us who we are to be? If a church does not locate itself where Christ is, can we actually know Christ's presence among us? Can we confess truthfully if we locate ourselves in other places and speak from out of other constructions of reality, and other places of reading the Scripture? If we celebrate the sacraments without a welcome to those with whom Christ sits, is it truly a right sacrament? What does it mean when the church does not shape its life around a public and political witness, and does not identify with and attest to Christ?

The church is both sinful and justified, and both justified and seeking to be sanctified. As Colin Gunton reminds us, human beings belong to a material and social dynamic that is marred by the fallenness of human beings. The church exists to reorient people, to form them

36. Volf, *After Our Likeness*, 148.

as a people who are oriented to perfection in Christ, but who live in a context where this eschatological hope is resisted. The church exists with the promise of redemption in Christ, a community that proclaims the forgiveness of sins, and which knows that through baptism it is already set on the way of Christ. "As the community of the last days living before the last days, the community of God's people exists to receive, through the action of the Spirit, a forward orientation, away from the realm of sin and death."[37] The marks of the church—*one*, *holy*, *catholic*, and *apostolic*—need to be interpreted relationally, and they need to be understood within the claims of justice and inclusion of those who are often marginalized. The framework for this conversation needs to be that of liberation theology. It needs to reflect James Cone's understanding of heresy, and of the relationship between confession and action: "Heresy here refers to any activity or teaching that contradicts the liberating truth of Jesus Christ. It is an action that denies the Lordship of Christ or a word that refuses to acknowledge his liberating presence in the struggle for freedom. Heresy is the refusal to speak the truth or to live the truth in the light of the One who is the Truth."[38] The church can only genuinely be the church when its words and actions reflect this liberating Christ, when words are translated into praxis, "the church living in the world on the basis of what it proclaims."[39] The church fails to be church when or where it is racist, aligned with oppressive powers, and is not concerned for the poor. As John Howard Yoder says, "*What it means to be the church is to be spoken of as a cause being implemented and not an ontology being realized.*"[40]

Conclusion

The church is the church when it locates itself where Christ is, thus genuinely gathering in Christ's name. In Australia the images of our life need to be of a servant community, open to diversity, and only determining its life in relation to Indigenous peoples.

37. Gunton, "The Church as a School of Virtue?" 225.

38. Cone, *God of the Oppressed*, 36.

39. Ibid.

40. Yoder, "Why Ecclesiology Is Social Ethics: Gospel Ethics versus the Wider Wisdom," in Yoder, *The Royal Priesthood*, 110 (italics original).

In Australia the church cannot be church unless Indigenous people are the church, and are not simply an object of the church's mission. This means being a community who are open to hearing God's voice in the world, and who know that that voice is heard in the lives of Indigenous people. It means helping people speak in ways that gives them space to flourish. To be a church in Australia is to change our social location, to disconnect ourselves from those with power, and to locate ourselves in the edges of the world.

What models and images will describe this church, and what marks will guarantee that we are the church? It is too early to say. It is not for one Second person to determine. There is a need for a long conversation, and much discussion between First and Second peoples in the church. For me, though, I think there is something to be gained from listening to Letty Russell's idea of the church as sanctuary,[41] and to Isabelle Graessle's reformulation of the marks of the church as "plurality, solidarity, contextuality and witness";[42] they provide a good beginning point for the conversation, particularly Graessle's view of solidarity as "a church whose existence is only justified when it cares for the marginalized, powerless, oppressed persons."[43]

41. Russell, "Hot-House Ecclesiology."
42. Graessle, "From Impasse to Passage," 28.
43. Ibid.

7

Reconciliation, Covenant, and Treaty

Introduction

AT THE HEART OF THIS BOOK HAS BEEN CONCERN FOR RELATIONSHIPS. In this brief chapter I want to touch on some of the conversations and movements in Australia that are concerned to reassess and change relationships between First and Second peoples. There will be some overlap, and revisiting and spelling out of earlier assumptions. This chapter reminds us of how easy it is, even with the best of intentions, to seek to control relationships and outcomes and to avoid the more equal and communal understanding that is found in the Christian understanding of the Trinitarian God.

Among the more important conversations that are occurring are

- The movement for reconciliation, which is about local and broader social relationships and understandings.

- The covenant that exists within the Uniting Church in Australia (UCA) between the United Aboriginal and Islander Christian Conference (UAICC) and other parts of the church, and the way the meaning of that covenant is constantly being negotiated.

- The movement for a treaty, which is about relationships in the political arena of the nation, including citizenship, and sovereignty.

- The movement for recognition of Indigenous peoples within the preamble to the Australian constitution.

- Suggestions that Australia Day should be moved from the day Europeans arrived to a day which all people could celebrate.

Each of these movements raises the issues of how relationships are named, how the past and its impact on the present are acknowledged, and how present relationships are made more just and inclusive. In this chapter I wish to reflect on reconciliation, covenant, and treaty.

Three Movements

Reconciliation

Reconciliation has to do with the healing of broken relationship, with enabling people to live together in peace and mutual well-being. It has to do with the way a people deal with past and present things that have harmed their relationship, with acknowledgement, forgiveness, and justice.

In the decade before the centenary of federation in Australia in 2001, there was concern that there should be an improvement in relationships between Indigenous and other Australians. It was a concern that grew out of a mixture of real goodwill and the pragmatic desire of some politicians to ensure that the celebrations were not marred by protest. In 1991 the Commonwealth Parliament agreed to establish the Council for Aboriginal Reconciliation and a formal reconciliation process. After ten years of encouraging the process, the council established Reconciliation Australia as a nongovernment, not-for-profit foundation to continue the work. The foundation identifies examples of reconciliation in action and promotes them so that others can add their support.

Broadly speaking, the movement for reconciliation seeks to promote the just recognition of Indigenous people as First peoples of this country, and to seek their full participation in Australian society. It encourages education and greater understanding in order to build better relationships and to break down the racism and stereotypes that often shape relationships. It has actively supported the need for an apology to the Stolen Generation. It is also working for constitutional change that offers real recognition of and support for Indigenous Australians.

Covenant

In 1988 the relatively new UAICC and the assembly of the UCA entered into a covenant as an expression of the relationship that should exist within the church. The covenant expressed a commitment to a relationship that would enable the UAICC to have oversight of ministry with

Indigenous people, and share in the struggle for a more just and equitable society. The covenant event involved the national president of the UCA reading a statement that was an act of truth telling and repentance, and which placed this covenant within God's covenant with humanity in Christ. Later in that same meeting, the chairperson of the UAICC made a gracious but honest response that called the invasion of Australia a disruption of God's plan, and indicated what Indigenous people could bring to a more honest and equal relationship. He reminded people that this was a starting point, and it needed to be translated into practical expressions of justice and love.[1]

A covenant is an agreement entered into by two or more parties in order that they might achieve certain common goals and build new relationships. It names the parties and sets out the terms of their present relationship. The covenant within the UCA seeks to build on our mutual life in Jesus Christ. It is concerned to bind people together in mutual commitment to Christ, and to call each of the partners to certain obligations and responsibilities. It challenges the wider church and its councils to build relationships with Indigenous people that involve a genuine sharing of resources and decision-making authority, and that builds relationships of mutual respect.

Treaty

As was made clear in chapter 1, the invasion and occupation of Australia involved a denial of the rights and sovereignty of Indigenous peoples. Indigenous people were no longer allowed to exercise control over their land or to administer their own laws. They were not recognized as people with rights and identity as separate peoples. In Australia no treaty was made with Indigenous people that would have recognized them as a people and spelled out their rights in society.

The first demand for a treaty came from the Larrikia people, whose land covers the town of Darwin in the Northern Territory. In March 1972 they sent a petition to the federal government, which, among other things, sought a treaty to suit each tribe.[2] The prime minister replied in

1. Both these covenant documents can be found in Bos and Thompson, *Theology for Pilgrims*, 631–40.

2. The words of the petition are reproduced in Wright, *We Call for a Treaty*, 15. She provides an excellent account of the history of the call for a treaty.

June 1972 and put forward a position that has been part of the official construction of worlds in Australia since invasion: Indigenous people were British subjects, and it would be inappropriate to negotiate with them as if they were foreign powers, and it was too difficult to know with whom to negotiate a treaty.[3] In April 1979 the National Aboriginal Conference (whose members were elected by Indigenous people) unanimously called for a treaty to be negotiated between Indigenous people and the Australian government. They did so in response to a court decision of that month which upheld an 1883 Privy Council decision that Australia was not acquired by conquest but was peacefully annexed. The implication in the court case was to deny that Indigenous people were a sovereign people who owned land that could not be taken from them without compensation.[4]

Treaties have to do with assertions of sovereignty. The United Nations, for example, defines a treaty as an international agreement made between states (where the issue of sovereignty is fairly well settled), although this seems more restrictive than the past practice of countries' making treaties with tribal groups. The assumption behind these latter treaties was that even if they were not nation-states, they were self-governing peoples and did claim dominion over a certain piece of land.

The proposal for a treaty in Australia is based on continuing claims to sovereignty and, thus the right to self-determination in regard to the political future, laws, land, and resources of Indigenous people. It is a claim to a recognized place within the structures of power and authority in this country.

The proposal for a treaty is not a unique issue to Australia. It is one that is being faced by many nations founded on the land of indigenous and native peoples. For example, a Royal Commission in Canada suggested that a new relationship was only possible as Aboriginal peoples were recognized as self-governing peoples with a unique place in Canada.[5] The way forward, they recommended, would include a treaty process, and recognition of Aboriginal nations and governments, and recognition of an Aboriginal order of government. It recognized that

3. Ibid.

4. For an account of this case, see ibid., 74–76.

5. The Royal Commission released its final report, "The Report of the Royal Commission on Aboriginal Peoples," in November 1996.

a significant percentage of Aboriginal people in Canada live in urban areas, which raises new issues about urban self-government. Part of the reason for the recommendations of the Royal Commission was that Aboriginal and treaty rights were entrenched in the Constitution Act of 1982, but these rights were not defined, and the struggle for the important right of self-determination has not been won. There are three central demands being made by Aboriginal peoples in Canada, which reflect the concerns that are raised in discussions around treaty in Australia:

- The right to be distinctive peoples; to resist the pressures to assimilate into the dominant culture; and to reclaim language, culture, and identity.

- The right to an adequate land base that will allow people—urban and rural—to give expression to their special relationship with the land. This means access to resources to develop and sustain a viable place in the economy.

- The right to self-determination, to shape their own future in a free and responsible way.

The Theological Landscape

The three issues raise a similar set of questions for the theological landscape:

- What is the proper relationship between reconciliation and justice?

- Should people not simply forget the issues from the past, offer forgiveness, and move on?

- Are present relationships simply the result of misunderstanding, or is there real wrongdoing in this situation?

- How do Second peoples approach these issues when they are the offending party and are not the ones who can forgive or decide what reconciliation should look like?

As well as these four common concerns, there are two issues of particular concern to covenant, and treaty:

- What is the theological foundation for covenant in the church?

- How does the church justify, theologically, the sovereignty of the state and its relationship to the sovereignty of God in the face of the challenge of treaty?

Reconciliation and Justice

Reconciliation lies at the heart of the Christian gospel. For example, 2 Corinthians 5:18–19 says: "All this [the new creation] is from God, who reconciled us to himself through Christ, and has given us the ministry of reconciliation; that is, in Christ God was reconciling the world to himself, not counting their trespasses against them, and entrusting the message of reconciliation to us."

The difficulty in the tradition of the church is that this reconciliation between God and humankind has often been left as just that—an issue between individuals and God that does not have social meaning. As Miroslav Volf says: "'Souls' are reconciled with God and individual persons are reconciled with one another, but the wider social world, ridden by strife, is left more or less to its own devises."[6] In this situation some Christians argue that the first priority is to get people to reconcile with God rather than worry about reconciliation between First and Second peoples in Australia.

There are other Christians who believe that the pursuit of reconciliation depends on the prior task of gaining justice. If the point is a new community in which people can live well together, then those who have been oppressed must be liberated first. Truly oppressed and abused people cannot be reconciled until people stop abusing them, and make amends for the past.

Volf suggests that this dichotomy between reconciliation and justice is unhelpful. Both are needed, but, in Volf's opinion, justice and liberation are not simply tasks that precede reconciliation or can be independent of it, but are "indispensable aspects of a more overarching agenda of reconciliation."[7] Reconciliation is the centre of the Christian faith, and liberation can only be the central action when there is manifest evil, and it is clearly on one side; and this is rarely the case. Justice

---

6. Volf, "The Social Meaning of Reconciliation," 162.
7. Ibid.

must be seen as an indispensible dimension of reconciliation, the goal of which is a new community founded in love.[8]

I think Volf is right, but there is a danger in suggesting that evil is rarely on one side. It is tempting for those with power, for those who have actually harmed and oppressed others to want to share the blame. People who abuse young girls try to suggest that they led them on, and rapists use the excuse that the victim "led them on." The issue is not that liberation should not be a first task, but that it is not an end in itself, for the goal is reconciliation and a new community.

There is an enormous difficulty in getting the Australian church to see that the suffering and dispossession of Indigenous people is not simply an ethical issue, but one about God. In part this is because of an ongoing denial of or a refusal to recognize the extent of the suffering. There is an unwillingness to allow for the reality of suffering to touch peoples' worlds in a way that challenges that world.

Where we speak from in this conversation is crucial. Are we observers, well-meaning people who wish to describe and "fix," or are we those who share life with those who suffer? It seems to me that the concern in Western theology for the suffering of God, and for an end to a theology of glory, often arises among a people and a church with power. It is an attempt to challenge the way a God of power has been used to support our power, and to encourage the church to share with God who suffers with the poor. The danger is that the image of the suffering, passive, accepting Christ can be used to justify the quiet submission of suffering people (women or the poor), who are then encouraged to find their life in the next world. Feminist writers remind us of how easily the church has spoken of the suffering of Jesus, and of the expectation that Christians could therefore suffer as well. They remind us that most of this good Christian suffering is done by women and others without power. "By emphasizing the mortal suffering of a beaten, scourged and defeated Christ as well as a spiritualized salvation in the other world, the Christian message was used to legitimize the colonial order by pacifying the people."[9]

There can be no reconciliation in Australia without justice, and not as an end in itself, but as the foundation for a new community. There

8. Ibid., 163.

9. Kwok, *Introducing Asian Feminist Theology*, 83.

can be no efforts to apportion or share blame or to place responsibility for what happens on Indigenous peoples. Racism, injustice, and abuse of power are issues for Second peoples to own, and deal with themselves.

Forgiving and Forgetting

In *Exclusion and Embrace*, in which he seeks to wrestle in very personal ways with how he loves the neighbor (Serbs) who killed his people (Croatians), Miroslav Volf deals with the issue of evil.[10] He insists that there cannot be change and easy forgiveness; there can be no quick fixes, and no pretence that things are all right. Evil must be named, and those who do evil must be confronted. Only then are reconciliation, forgiveness, and new beginnings possible.

Second peoples cannot say to Indigenous peoples that it is their Christian duty to forgive, or that Indigenous peoples would be better off just forgetting what has happened in the past. Forgiveness is not forgetting the past but allowing that story a different place in our life. For that to be possible, history must be acknowledged and honored. It is to say, "You are right. This happened, and it was wrong, and I want to build a different future." It is to understand that the past shapes both the social and political possibilities in people's lives, and the narrative framework in which they people live and make sense of what happens. Those with power, those who have harmed others, must act to change both the lived reality and the meaning-situation that shapes hope and human well-being.

All We Need Is Education

The liberal political and religious assumption is that people are basically good and well meaning, and that all they lack is understanding. If people can be brought into contact with other people, if they can be given an opportunity to learn, then everything will be all right.

The Christian tradition says that human life is broken, and distorted because people live in a broken relationship with God. The Bible does not describe people this way because it wishes them to feel bad. The Bible speaks of evil because this is its experience. It offers a theological explanation for what people know to be true: there is an

---

10. Volf, *Exclusion and Embrace*.

enormous amount of violence, cruelty, abuse, pain, and suffering in the world. Lives are distorted by past abuse, lack of love, or betrayal.

It is important that people meet and share their lives. It is particularly important that Second peoples hear the story of First peoples firsthand. But this is not enough. People need to be able to name the past for what it was, to own the injustice, and to *act* to help put it right.

Consider the account of Paul's conversion in Acts 9. Paul has set himself against the infant church and, without knowing it, against the exalted Christ whose body this is. On the road to Damascus Paul is encountered by God who names this injustice: "Saul Saul, why do you persecute me?" (Acts 9:4). Paul asks who is speaking to him, and the voice says it is Jesus. Now here is the crunch. Will Paul be punished and destroyed, or simply allowed to move on? The answer is neither. God names the injustice, challenges Saul to tell God why he would do this thing, and confronts Paul with a new future in the very act of offering reconciliation and a new beginning. The putting right that was demanded of Saul, as he became Paul, was that he would now build, and defend, the very church that he had set out to destroy. He could not change the past, but he could be part of a different future.

How Do Second People Enter This Conversation?

This is a difficult conversation for Second peoples, for it is our natural inclination to want to control the agenda and to describe the issue from our perspective. We want to decide what reconciliation, covenant, and treaty are all about, and to suggest how Indigenous people should respond. But this is a conversation in which we are guests, in which it is not about what we want, but what Indigenous people want. Our entry point is not, as it usually is, whether we should forgive people, or punish them, but can we repent, make amends and change our lives? The best we can do is to prepare ourselves to listen, to be able to hear hard things that we do not like to hear, and to remain silent rather than to immediately defend ourselves. It is the silence that waits for the invitation to speak rather than always claiming our right to contribute, and shape the conversation. There is a challenge to humility that is not easy to deal with.

The Theological Foundation for Covenant[11]

If reconciliation is at the heart of the gospel, it is because relationship sits at the heart of the Trinitarian God. The Trinitarian nature of God reveals to us that the heart of God is personal life in relationship rather than solitary isolation or self-contained, unfeeling existence. As Jürgen Moltmann suggests, drawing on the work of the fourth-century Cappadocians,[12] the Trinitarian God is best described as a social being whose unity is found in the eternal *perichoresis*, or dancing, of the Father, Son, and Holy Spirit. The unity within God is found in a changing, emerging, celebrating relationship that alters through the dance as God moves around those who share the floor. This communication within the Trinity is free from domination, and the three persons "have everything in common apart from their personal characteristics."[13] As the Council of Florence (1442) said, "Because of this unity the Father is fully in the Son, fully in the Holy Spirit; the Son is fully in the Father, fully in the Holy Spirit; the Holy Spirit is fully in the Father, fully in the Son."[14]

The world exists because the love that holds the Trinity into the dance bursts out into the need for another life that is not God. God desires an "other" with whom God can share life. It is God who sustains the world, who continues to speak a word that keeps the world going, and who also brings salvation, healing, and renewal.

The model for relationships in the church is the communal, relational, mutual indwelling life of God, a relationship that finds expression in covenant. The foundation of the covenant relationship is the claim that we are communally, rather than individually, a reflection of this social life of the Trinity. The biblical foundation for covenant is found in God's act of creation, in God's promise to Noah that nothing would ever destroy the earth (Gen 10:14–17), in the call of Abraham (Genesis 12), and in the covenant with the people taken from Egypt, and called to be a new people in a new land (Deuteronomy 7–8). Each involves a

---

11. This section on the theology of the covenant is based on an earlier work, which I wrote with John Rickard, and which is a resource paper for use within the UCA. It is called "Theological Foundations for a Covenant," and is available on the assembly Web site: http://assembly.uca.org.au.

12. Gregory of Nyssa, Gregory of Nazianzus, and Basil of Caesarea. Moltmann's work is found in, for example, *History and the Triune God*.

13. Moltmann, *History and the Triune God*, xv.

14. Quoted in ibid.

promise from God, a call to relationship, and the desire that people live a distinctive way of life. The ultimate expression of covenant was that renewed by Jesus Christ, who called all human beings to be sons and daughters who live inclusively and equally (e.g., Gal 3:28).

The theological foundation for a covenanted life is the social nature of our being in God's image that allows for diversity and seeks joyful and open interaction. We do not begin in unity and then have to argue for difference, but we begin in our differences with the assurance that we are bound together through a shared relation with God. It is neither our sameness nor our organization likeness that provides the basis for our relationship, but a common commitment to explore together our relationship with God, and what that means for the wholeness of the earth and God's people.

At the heart of God's Trinitarian life and the life of Jesus Christ is God's generous reaching out into the life of the creation. It is the story of incarnation, of becoming a particular life among a particular people. The very idea of incarnation is concerned for embodiment in a particular time and place. The incarnation is about Jesus being human, and thus is about the sociocultural and political particularity of Jesus's life. It is about God's deep sympathy with human weakness and struggle, situated in a particular geographical, social, and political location. The life and death of Christ is an act of unconditional participation by God in the world. God is *our* God and has accommodated Godself to human weakness and struggle. The event of the cross is not simply an additional or special event; rather it is the culmination of God's movement towards creation. The divine compassion of God is a movement of absolute grace and freedom, a turning to a world that God believes has such value and is so good and beautiful, that it is worth dying for.

The incarnation points to the embodiment that is essential to human life and to the way that embodiment fits into the purposes of God. We cannot be human apart from location, community, place, and a particular social situation. Like all people, the Indigenous peoples of Australia embody in one place and particular situation the image of God. Covenant is not one people coming with the gift of Christ, and the other coming empty handed to receive what the other has to offer. God was in this land with Indigenous people and is recognized in the Dreaming and the law and the lives of the Indigenous community. There can be no theological equivalent of *terra nullius*, no claim that this land was empty and unoccupied by God. There can be no claim that God was brought to Australia by the churches; rather, we need to discover what it means to affirm the presence of God in this land from the beginning of creation.[15]

Hospitality

Consideration of the relationship between the UAICC and other parts of the UCA has generally been conceived of in terms of organizational unity. Even covenant is often understood around matters of polity and structure. However, the previous section suggested that relationships in the church are shaped by the relational heart of the Trinitarian God, what at this point I would call divine hospitality.

Hospitality is a central feature of the ministry of Jesus, as he reaches out, and welcomes into his company those who are marginalized and excluded. He gives expression to this hospitality in meals, in care for the ill and unclean, and in being open to the touch of those considered to be untouchable. It is a hospitality that breaks down barriers and is open to the other.

Brendan Byrne suggests that Luke's gospel sees the whole of Jesus's life as the entry of God into the world as a guest. The issue Jesus raises for people as they meet him is, "how will they receive this one who makes himself vulnerable by coming as a guest rather than as host?" "The crucial point is that those who do receive him find that he brings them into a much wider sphere of hospitality: the 'hospitality of God.' The One who comes as a visitor and guest in fact becomes *host* and offers a hospitality in which human beings and, potentially, the entire world, can become truly human, be at home, can *know* salvation in the depths of their heart."[16]

The church's life and relationships are to be modeled on the dancing life of the Trinity and on hospitality. It is about being open to the other, with the hope and expectation that as we offer others welcome, they will become the hosts who open for us a new way of being in the world. We are not doing a favor for others, but allowing the one who is visitor to be host. Indeed, in Australia one of the challenges for Second

15. See the discussion in chapter 4 for suggestions about the way we might speak about God, the Word, and other religions.

16. Byrne, *Hospitality of God*, 4.

peoples is to recognize that they are not the hosts but guests—uninvited guests—on Aboriginal land. The challenge is how we become guests, and allow Indigenous people to properly be hosts.

The Theological Claim to Sovereignty

The issue of treaty challenges the assumption of the modern nation-state that it is the one focus and source of sovereignty, and that the only loyalty must be to the state. It suggests the possibility of other forms of sovereignty and loyalty. Treaty actually raises the same issue faced by Christians in this time: can people be loyal members of a nation and still offer their absolute loyalty to God? Theologically the issue is, how does the church speak of the sovereignty of the state *vis-a-vis* the sovereignty of God? Is the state a body that exercises God's lordship in God's stead, or is the state's lordship always relative to what people owe God? Is there a place for multiple and at times contested loyalties, and is sovereignty exercised centrally, and hierarchically?

I suggested in an earlier chapter that one of the things that had shaped theology was the shift in the relationship between the church and state, and between discipleship and citizenship. Part of that change was from the confession "Jesus is Lord" as a confession over against the claims of emperor and empire to the claim that the emperor is also lord, one who exercises lordship on behalf of God. In this transition, language about God changed, and God is now called both Lord and Father. However, this is not the intimate father that Jesus spoke of, but one who is a patriarch of the family. The Reformers drew their model for rule in the emerging state from the relationships they saw in the family, and this was a male-headed household ruled hierarchically. God the Father was the model for families and for the state. The model of God the Father legitimated hierarchical authority.[17] This understanding of power fits very well with the claim of the modern nation-state that all authority rests in the state, and ultimate loyalty must be given to that state.

The doctrine of the Trinity will not allow this easy merging of the idea of God as Lord and Father. Rather, while each person of the Trinity is fully in the others, yet there is one who is Father, and one who is

17. Moltmann, *History and the Triune God*, 7–8.

the Lord Jesus Christ, who expresses the liberating rule of the Trinity.[18] That is, the Father cannot be made easily into a lord who becomes the foundation and model for authority and unity in family and state.

The discussion of Treaty challenges the assumption of the nation-state that there is a necessary unity found within the authority of the state, and that all diversity must find its centre in that unified state. Treaty suggests that there is space for a different form of sovereignty, and that unity is found in a more complex set of relationships

How Do We Move Forward?

Reconciliation, covenant, and treaty and are all contested conversations, for they call people to own the history of this country, and to consider the foundation for present relationships. They challenge assumptions about where power rests, who controls relationships, and where people are socially located. They are conversations that challenge Second peoples because they demand more than polite words, and expressions of good intent. For example, many Indigenous people are skeptical of the reconciliation conversations, for they appear to be about making Second peoples feel good rather than actually achieving justice as the foundation for real reconciliation.

Language about Trinity and hospitality challenges the way we see power, and the way we understand the relationships that should exist between people. The issue being raised is whether Second peoples can actually share power and resources, and allow for relationships that they do not control. Language about reconciliation and justice suggests that the past must be named and not simply ignored, and that goal is new community. The central issue, the one that runs right through this book, is how Second peoples give up control of relationships and help build more mutual and more equal lives. The issue is how we place all forms of sovereignty and control within the sovereign, serving lordship of Jesus Christ and our Trinitarian God.

18. Ibid., 7.

Postscript

What Have We Learned from This Journey?

THE ART OF THEOLOGY IS CIRCULAR, A MOVEMENT THROUGH CONTEXT, methodology, tradition, and belief and the practices of the Christian life. Depending on what we are doing, what our situation and context demand of us, or on how we conceive of the theological task, we enter the circle at different points. The point is, though, that having moved around the circle, we reenter our starting point but as different people to the first time. Hopefully we have been changed by the journey, and we enter the task in a different way.

I was putting the finishing touches to this book on Australia Day, January 26, 2009. Each year at this time, a person is declared Australian of the Year, and this year it was Professor Mick Dodson—Indigenous scholar, activist, and a commissioner for the Stolen Generation report, *Bringing Them Home*. One of his first actions after being named Australian of the Year for 2009 was to raise the question of whether January 26 (the day the First Fleet arrived in Australia in 1788) was the best day to celebrate Australia Day, given that many Indigenous people call this day invasion day. He didn't say the date should shift, and he didn't suggest other dates, but he simply tried to start a conversation. The prime minister quickly stepped in and said that his government would not contemplate a change of date.

Conversations in Australia about our history and identity are difficult ones. There is a fear of open discussion, a refusal to acknowledge the seriousness of Indigenous concerns, and a willingness by governments to use their power to avoid difficult and embarrassing issues. There is a tension between very well-intentioned speeches about reconciliation, recognition, and forgiveness, and the refusal to actually engage with issues that concern Indigenous people. Even the best intentions get caught within a framework of control, marginalization, and barely concealed racism.

Theology always faces the danger of idealism, of being convinced that it is ideas that shape reality. This is so even in contextual theology, and as I come to the end of this book, I am aware that any ongoing conversation needs to be more aware of the way ideas serve social interest and are shaped by them. I need to be more aware of practices.

It is hard to escape the sense in our culture that everything will be alright, that progress will be made if we just have the goodwill and desire to learn. It is hard to name evil and broken-ness in our live.

There are four things I have learned, or learned afresh and in new ways, as I have worked in this book. First, it is so very hard to see what has been declared as "normal." It shapes our perceptions, but far too often we are not even aware. We need to keep listening for voices that remind us that our normal is not necessarily everybody's normal.

Second, part of what is considered normal is the way we see race in this country, and the way that being white and male are the measure for everything else. Even when we try really hard, even when we want to do the very best things, we find ourselves caught in a history of racism. We need to be more aware of, more willing to own, the residual racism in our lives.

Third, it is never easy for Second peoples to put aside our interests, or even to acknowledge them. It is certainly difficult to give up control, to get past the desire to rush to right answers and correct conclusions. I may have erred in offering too few conclusions, particularly in part 2 of this book, but I wanted to clear the ground, to identify the issues, to suggest an agenda, rather than rush to a final position. The next stage must be a more shared journey.

And, finally, at the heart of struggles over relationships is social location, who we genuinely share our lives with. Social location shapes what we see, what interests we protect, and where we look for God. I have learned again how far I need to move if I am to sit with the living Christ on the margins of this country.

I hope you find yourself in a different place at the end of this book than the beginning. I hope you will contribute to this journey, join these same discussions from within your place, and broaden the search for a Second peoples' theology.

Chris Budden
January 31, 2009

Bibliography

Indigenous Authors

(It is not always possible to know who is an Indigenous author. I apologize to any person whom I have not recognized in the appropriate way.)

Blyton, Greg, et al. *Wannin Thanbarran: A History of Aboriginal and European Contact in Muswellbrook and the Upper Hunter Valley.* Muswellbrook: Muswellbrook Shire Council Aboriginal Reconciliation Committee, 2004.

Broome, Richard. *Aboriginal Australians: Black Responses to White Dominance 1788-2001.* 3rd ed. Crows Nest, NSW: Allen & Unwin, 2001.

———. "Aboriginal Victims and Voyagers, Confronting Frontier Myths." *Journal of Australian Studies* 42 (1994) 70–77.

Central Land Council. *From the Grassroots: Feedback from Traditional Landowners and Community Members on the Australian Government Intervention.* Unpublished Briefing Paper (19 December 2007). Online: http://www.clc.org.au/media/From_the_Grassroots_Briefing.pdf/.

Chapman, Valerie, and Peter Read, editors. *Terrible Hard Biscuits: A Reader in Aboriginal History.* St. Leonards, NSW: The Journal of Aboriginal History and Allen & Unwin, 1996.

Dingo, Sally. *Dingo: The Story of Our Mob.* Milsons Point, NSW: Random House, 1998.

Gillespie, Waratah Rose. *About Aboriginal Sovereignty: Sending a Message, Seeking New Pathways.* Canberra: Yearly Meeting Indigenous Concerns Committee of the Religious Society of Friends (Quakers) in Australia, 2005.

Gondarra, Djiniyini. "Overcoming the Captivities of the Western Church Context." In *The Cultured Pearl: Australian Readings in Cross-Cultural Theology and Mission,* edited Jim Houston, 176–82. Melbourne: Victorian Council of Churches, 1986.

———. *Series of Reflections of Aboriginal Theology.* Darwin: Bethel Presbytery, Northern Synod Uniting Church of Australia, 1986.

Langford Ginibi, Ruby. *Don't Take Your Love to Town.* St. Lucia, Queensland: University of Queensland Press, 2007.

Langton, Marcia. "Real Change for Real People." *Australian,* January 26, 2008. Online: http://www.theaustralian.news.com.au/story/0,25197,23109644-28737,00.html/.

————. "Trapped in the Aboriginal Reality Show." In *Griffith Review: Re-Imagining Australia* 19 (2008) 17pp. Online: http://www3.griffithreview.edu.au/.

Meehan, Donna. *It Is No Secret: The Story of a Stolen Child.* Milsons Point, NSW: Random House Australia, 2000.

Miller, James. *Koori, A Will to Win: The Heroic Resistance, Survival & Triumph of Black Australia.* Sydney: Angus & Robertson, 1985.

Morgan, Sally. *My Place.* Freemantle: Freemantle Arts Centre Press, 1987.

Morgan, Sally, et al., editors. *Heartsick for Country. Stories of Love, Spirit and Creation.* Freemantle: Freemantle Press, 2008.

Mudrooroo. *Us Mob: History, Culture, Struggle: An Introduction to Indigenous Australia.* Sydney: Angus & Robertson, 1995.

Parbury, Nigel. *Survival: A History of Aboriginal Life in New South Wales.* Sydney: Ministry of Aboriginal Affairs, 1986.

Pascoe, Bruce. *Convincing Ground: Learning to Fall in Love with Your Country.* Canberra: Aboriginal Studies Press, 2007.

Pattel-Gray, Anne. *The Great White Flood: Racism in Australia; Critically Appraised from an Aboriginal Historico-Theological Viewpoint.* American Academy of Religion Cultural Criticism Series. Atlanta: Scholars, 1998.

————. editor. *Aboriginal Spirituality: Past, Present, Future.* Blackburn, Vic.: HarperCollins Religious, 1996.

Rainbow Spirit Elders. *Rainbow Spirit Theology: Towards an Australian Aboriginal Theology.* 2nd edition. Hindmarsh, SA: AFT Press, 2007.

Thompson, David, editor. *Milbi Dabaar: A Resource Book.* North Cairns, Queensland: Wantulup-Bi-Buya College, 2004.

Wright, Judith. *We Call for a Treaty.* Sydney: Collins/Fontana, 1985.

History and Culture

Allen, Margaret Ellen. "Homely Stories and the Ideological Work of 'Terra Nullius'" In "Rezoning Australia." Special issue, *Journal of Australian Studies* 79 (2003) 105–15. St. Lucia, Queensland: Queensland University Press, 2003.

Arthur, Jay, "The Eighth Day of Creation." *Journal of Australian Studies* 61 (1999) 66–74.

Australian Institute of Criminology (Australian Government). "Crime Facts Info No. 88: Prison Custody Deaths 1982-2003." Online: http://www.aic.gov.au/publications/cfi/cfi088.html.

————. "Indigenous Justice in Australia: Indigenous Deaths in Custody." Online: http://www.aic.gov.au/topics/indigenous/cjs/dic.html

Bell, Diane. *Ngarrindjeri Wurruwarrin: A World That Is, Was, and Will Be.* North Melbourne, Vic.: Spinifex, 1998.

Brennan, Frank, et al. *Finding Common Ground: An Assessment of the Bases of Aboriginal Land Rights.* Revised edition. Blackburn, Vic.: Collins Dove, 1986.

Brock, Peggy. "Protecting Colonial Interests: Aborigines and Criminal Justice." *Journal of Australian Studies* 53 (1997) 120–29.

Buti, Antonio. *Sir Ronald Wilson: A Matter of Conscience.* Crawley, WA: University of Western Australia Press, 2007.

Chamberlin, J. Edward. *If This Is Your Land, Where Are Your Stories?: Re-Imagining Home and Sacred Space.* Cleveland: Pilgrim, 2003.

Chidester, David. *Savage Systems: Colonialism and Comparative Religion in Southern Africa.* Studies in Religion and Culture. Charlottesville: University Press of Virginia, 1996.

Cunneen, Chris. "Book Review: *Indigenous Deaths in Custody 1989 to 1996.*" *Indigenous Law Bulletin* 62 (1997) 26. Online: http://www.austlii.edu.au/au/journals/ILB/1997/62.html/.

Davis, Mike. *Late Victorian Holocausts: El Niño Famines and the Making of the Third World.* London: Verso, 2001.

Dodson, Mick. "Finally Their Voices Will Be Heard." *Sydney Morning Herald*, February 13, 2008. Online: http://www.theaustralian.news.com.au/story/0,25197,228885 52-16741,00.html/.

Francis, Mark. "Social Darwinism and the Construction of Institutional Racism in Australia." *Journal of Australian Studies* 50/51 (1996) 90–105.

Fredrickson, George M. *Racism: A Short History.* Foreword by Robert Manne. Carlton North, Vic.: Scribe, 2002.

Gelder, Ken, and Jane M. Jacobs. *Uncanny Australia: Sacredness and Identity in a Postcolonial Nation.* Carlton South, Vic.: Melbourne University Press, 1998.

Goodall, Heather. *Invasion to Embassy: Land in Aboriginal Politics in New South Wales, 1770–1972.* St. Leonards, NSW: Allen & Unwin, 1996.

Grant, Anna. "Imprisonment of Indigenous Women in Australia 1988–1998." *Indigenous Law Bulletin.* 30(1999). Online: http://reconciliation.org.au/nsw/education-kit/about/

Graubard, Stephen R., editor. *Australia: The Daedalus Symposium.* North Ryde, NSW: Angus & Robertson, 1985.

Grey, Anthony J. *Jabiluka: The Battle to Mine Australia's Uranium.* Melbourne: Text Publishing, 1994.

Harris, John W. *One Blood: 200 Years of Aboriginal Encounter with Christianity; A Story of Hope.* 2nd edition. Sutherland, NSW: Albatross, 1990.

Healey, Justin, editor. *Indigenous Australians and the Law.* Issues in Society. Thirroul, NSW: Spinney, 2007.

Hirst, J. B. *Sense & Nonsense in Australian History.* Agenda Series. Melbourne: Black, 2006.

Howard, John. Speech to the House of Representatives, 30 October 1996. *Parliamentary Debates*, House of Representatives. House of Representatives, Official Hansard, 30 October 1996. Thirty-eighth Parliament, First Session, Second Period. Canberra: Parliament of Australia, 1996. Online: http://www.aph.gov.au/Hansard/hansreps.htm#1996/dr30196.pdf/.

Hurley, Mary C., and Jim Wherrett. *The Report of the Royal Commission on Aboriginal People: Summary.* 2 August 2000. Online: http://www.parl.gc.ca/information/library/PRBpubs/prb9924-e.htm/.

Kenny, Robert. *The Lamb Enters the Dreaming: Nathanael Pepper & the Ruptured World.* Carlton North, Vic.: Scribe, 2007.

Krieg, Anthea S. "Aboriginal Incarceration: Health and Social Impacts." *Medical Journal of Australia* 84 (2006) 534–36.

MacIntyre, Stuart, and Anna Clark. *The History Wars.* New Updated edition. Carleton, Vic.: Melbourne University Press, 2004.

Manne, Robert, editor. *Whitewash: On Keith Windschuttle's Fabrication of Aboriginal History*. Agenda Series. Melbourne: Black, 2003.

Muecke, Stephen. *Textual Spaces: Aboriginality and Cultural Studies*. Communication and Culture Series. Kensington, NSW: University of New South Wales Press, 1992.

National Inquiry into the Separation of Aboriginal and Torres Strait Islander Children from their Families. *Bringing Them Home: Report of the National Inquiry into the Separation of Aboriginal and Torres Strait Islander Children from their Families*. Parliamentary paper (Australian Parliament) 1997, no. 128. Sydney: Human Rights and Equal Opportunity Commission, 1997.

Parry, Naomi. "Such a Longing: Black and White Children in Welfare in New South Wales and Tasmania, 1880–1940." PhD dissertation, University of New South Wales, 2007.

Patterson, Richard North. *Exile: A Novel*. New York: St. Martin's Paperbacks, 2007,

Pearson, Noel. "Drug Abusers Should Just Say Sorry." *Australian*, December 8, 2007. Online: http://www.theaustralian.news.com.au/story/0,25197,22887396 -7583,00.html/.

Radic, Therese. "The Song Lines of *Waltzing Matilda*." *Journal of Australian Studies* 49 (1996) 39–47.

Ramsey, Alan. "A Cynical Scratch, a Pustular Response." *The Sydney Morning Herald*, June 30, 2007, 35. Online: http://www.smh.com.au/news/opinion/a-cynical- scratch-a-pustular-response/2007/06/29/1182624168798.html?page=fullpage/.

———. "The True Story of Inaction Is on the Record." *The Sydney Morning Herald*, June 30, 2007, 35. Online: http://www.smh.com.au/news/opinion/a-cynical- scratch-a-pustular-response/2007/06/29/1182624168798.html?page=fullpage/.

Reconciliation Australia. "Apology to the 'Stolen Generations." Online: http://www .reconciliation.org.au/home/reconciliation-resources/qa-factsheets/apology/.

Reynolds, Henry. *Black Pioneers: How Aboriginal and Islander People Helped Build Australia*. Revised edition. Ringwood, Vic.: Penguin, 2000.

———. "Frontier History after Mabo." *Journal of Australian Studies* 49 (1996) 4–11.

———. *The Law of the Land*. Ringwood, Vic.: Penguin, 1987.

———. *The Other Side of the Frontier: An Interpretation of the Aboriginal Response to the Invasion and Settlement of Australia*. Townsville, Queensland: History Department James Cook University, 1981.

———. *Why Weren't We Told?: A Personal Search for the Truth about Our History*. Camberwell, Vic.: Viking, 1999.

Riddett, Lyn. "Thinking Again: Communities Which Lose Their Memory; The Construction of History in Settler Societies." *Journal of Australian Studies*. 44 (1995) 38–47.

Rosenbaum, Alan S., editor. *Is the Holocaust Unique? Perspectives on Comparative Genocide*. Boulder, CO: Westview, 1996.

Rothwell, Nicolas. "No Time for Dreaming." *Australian*, December 7, 2008. Online: http://www.theaustralian.news.com.au/story/0,25197,22887742-28737,00 .html/.

Summers, Anne. *Damned Whores and God's Police: The Colonization of Women in Australia*. Ringwood, Vic.: Penguin, 1976.

Thorp, Bill. "Frontiers of Discourse: Assessing Revisionist Australian Colonial Contact Historiography." *Journal of Australian Studies* 4 (1995) 34–45.

Toohey, Paul. "Last Drinks: The Impact of the Northern Territory Intervention." *Quarterly Essay* 30 (2008) 1–97.

"Time to Permit the Truth to Be Told: Shackling the Media Protects Child Abusers and Criminals." *The Australian*, December 8, 2007. Online: http://www.theaustralian .news.com.au/story/0,25197,22888552-16741,00.html/.

Trudgen, Richard Ian. *Why Warriors Lie Down & Die: Towards an Understanding of Why the Aboriginal People of Arnhem Land Face the Greatest Crisis in Health and Education since European Contact.* Darwin: Aboriginal Resource and Development Services Inc., 2000.

Wild, Rex, and Patricia Anderson. *Little Children Are Sacred: Report of the Northern Territory Board of Enquiry into the Protection of Aboriginal Children from Sexual Abuse.* Darwin: Government Printer of the Northern Territory, 2007. Online: http://www.nt.gov.au/dcm/inquirysaac/pdf/bipacsa_final_report.pdf/.

Wilson, Paul R. *Black Death, White Hands.* Revised edition. North Sydney: Allen & Unwin, 1985.

Windschuttle, Keith. "Don't Let Facts Spoil the Day." *The Australian*, February 9, 2008.

————. *The Fabrication of Aboriginal History.* Volume 1, *Van Dieman's Land 1803 –1847.* Sydney: Macleay, 2002.

Woolmington, Jean. "'Humble Artisans' and 'Untutored Savages.'" *Journal of Australian Studies* 16 (1985) 51–61.

Theology and Social Construction of Reality

Alston, Wallace M. Jr., and Michael Welker, editors. *Reformed Theology: Identity and Ecumenicity.* Grand Rapids: Eerdmans, 2003.

Asad, Talal. *Genealogies of Religion: Discipline and Reasons of Power in Christianity and Islam.* Baltimore: John Hopkins University Press, 1993.

Barth, Karl. *Church Dogmatics: A Selection.* With an Introduction by Helmut Gollwitzer. Translated and edited by G. W. Bromiley. New York: Harper & Row, 1962.

————. *Church Dogmatics. IV/3:1: The Doctrine of Reconciliation.* Edited by Geoffrey W. Bromley and T. F. Torrance. Edinburgh: T. & T. Clark, 1962.

————. *Evangelical Theology: An Introduction.* Translated by Grover Foley. New York: Holt, Rinehart and Winston, 1963.

————. *The Knowledge of God and the Service of God according to the Teaching of the Reformation, Recalling the Scottish Confession of 1560.* The Gifford Lectures 1937–1938. Translated by J. L. M. Haire and Ian Henderson. London: Hodder & Stoughton, 1955.

Baum, Gregory, editor. *The Twentieth Century: A Theological Overview.* Maryknoll NY: Orbis, 1999.

Belo, Fernando. *A Materialist Reading of the Gospel of Mark.* Translated by Matthew J. O'Connell. Maryknoll, NY: Orbis, 1981.

Berger, Peter L. *Pyramids of Sacrifice: Political Ethics and Social Change*. Harmonds-worth: Penguin, 1977.

Berger, Peter L., and Thomas Luckmann. *The Social Construction of Reality: A Treatise in the Sociology of Knowledge*. Harmondsworth: Penguin, 1967.

Bevans, Stephen B. *Models of Contextual Theology*. Rev. ed. Faith and Cultures Series. Maryknoll, NY: Orbis, 1992.

Bieler, Andre. "Gradual Awareness of Social, Economic Problems (1750–1900)." In *Separation Without Hope? Essays on the Relation between the Church and the Poor during the Industrial Revolution and the Western Colonial Expansion*, edited by Julio de Santa Ana, 3–29. Commission on the Churches' Participation in Development. Geneva, Switzerland: World Council of Churches, 1978.

Bonhoeffer, Dietrich. *Christology*. Introduced by Edwin H. Robertson. Translated by John Bowden. London: Collins, 1966.

———. *Letters and Papers from Prison*. Edited by Eberhard Bethge. Translated by Reginald Fuller et al. Enlarged Edition. London: SCM, 1971.

Bos, Rob, and Geoff Thompson, editors. *Theology for Pilgrims: Selected Theological Documents of the Uniting Church in Australia*. Sydney: Uniting Church Press, 2008.

Brown, Delwin, et al., editors. *Converging on Culture: Theologians in Dialogue with Cultural Analysis and Criticism*. The American Academy of Religion Reflection and Theory in the Study of Religion Series. Oxford: Oxford University Press, 2001.

Brownson, James V. et al. *StormFront: The Gospel of God*. The Gospel and Our Culture Series. Grand Rapids: Eerdmans, 2003.

Brueggemann, Walter. *The Prophetic Imagination*. Philadelphia: Fortress, 1978.

———. *Theology of the Old Testament: Testimony, Dispute, Advocacy*. Minneapolis: Fortress, 1997.

Brueggemann, Walter, and George W. Stroup, editors. *Many Voices, One God: Being Faithful in a Pluralistic World; In Honor of Shirley Guthrie*. Louisville: Westminster John Knox, 1998.

Budden, Chris. "Discipleship and Citizenship: A Growing Source of Tension. *Uniting Church Studies* 14 (2008) 24.

———. "Exploring Contextual Theology in Australia in Dialogue with Indigenous People." *International Journal of Public Theology* 2 (2008) 292–312.

———. "The Location of God, Theories of the Atonement and 'Redemptive' Violence." In *Validating Violence Violating Faith?: Religion, Scripture and Violence*, edited by William T. Emilsen and John T. Squires, 155–71. Adelaide: ATF Press, 2008.

———. "A Response to Aveling's 'Dietrich Bonhoeffer's Christology.'" *Colloquium* 16 (1984) 39–42.

Budden, Chris, and John Rickard. "Theological Foundations for a Covenant as an Expression of the Relationship between the UAICC and other parts of the Uniting Church." Discussion Document prepared for the national Assembly of the Uniting Church." Online: http://www.victas.uca.org.au/main .php?pg=download&id=236293/

Byrne, Brendan. *The Hospitality of God: A Reading of Luke's Gospel*. Strathfield, NSW: St Pauls, 2000.

Calvin, John. *Institutes of the Christian Religion*. Translated by Henry Beveridge. London: Clarke, 1962.

Cannon, Katie Geneva. *Black Womanist Ethics*. American Academy of Religion Academy Series 60. Atlanta: Scholars, 1988.

Carroll, Seforosa. "Who is Jesus Christ For Me in Australia: A Reflection on Virginia Fabellar's *Christology from an Asian Woman's Perspective*." In *God's Image* 19 (2000) 58–64.

Cassell, Eric J. *The Nature of Suffering and the Goals of Medicine*. New York: Oxford University Press, 1991.

Cavanaugh, William T. "'A Fire Strong Enough to Consume the House': The Wars of Religion and the Rise of the State." *Modern Theology* 11(1995) 397–420.

———. *Theopolitical Imagination: Discovering the Liturgy as a Political Act in an Age of Global Consumerism*. London: T. & T. Clark, 2002.

Commission on Faith and Order. *The Nature and Purpose of the Church: A Stage on the Way to a Common Statement*. Faith and Order Paper No. 181. Geneva: World Council of Churches, 1998.

Cone, James H. *God of the Oppressed*. New York: Seabury, 1975.

Darragh, Neil. *Doing Theology Ourselves: A Guide to Research and Action*. Auckland, NZ: Accent, 1995.

Davis, Charles. *Theology and Political Society*. The Hulsean Lectures in the University of Cambridge: 1978. Cambridge: Cambridge University Press, 1980.

De La Torre, Miguel A. *Doing Christian Ethics from the Margins*. Maryknoll, NY: Orbis, 2004.

Dubuoc, Christian, and Casiano Floristán, editors. *Where Is God? A Cry of Human Distress*. London: SCM, 1992; and *Concilium* 4 (1992).

Dutney, Andrew. *Playing God: Ethics and Faith*. East Melbourne: HarperCollinsReligious, 2001.

Emilsen, Susan, and William W. Emilsen, editors. *Mapping the Landscape: Essays in Australian and New Zealand Christianity. Festschrift in Honour of Professor Ian Breward*. American University Studies 193. New York: Lang, 2000.

Fanon, Frantz. *Black Skin, White Masks*. Translated by Charles Lam Markmann. New York: Grove Weidenfeld, 1991.

Fiddes, Paul S. *Participating in God: A Pastoral Doctrine of the Trinity*. London: Darton, Longman & Todd, 2000.

Flannery, Austin, editor. *The Conciliar and Post Conciliar Documents: Vatican Council II*. Signpost Books. Dublin: Dominican, 1975.

Goosen, Gideon C. *Australian Theologies: Themes and Methodologies into the Third Millennium*. Strathfield, NSW: St Pauls, 2000.

Graessle, Isabelle. "From Impasse to Passage: Reflections on the Church." *Ecumenical Review* 53 (2001) 25–35.

Gunton, Colin. "The Church as a School of Virtue? Human Formation in Trinitarian Framework." In *Faithfulness and Fortitude: In Conversation with the Theological Ethics of Stanley Hauerwas*, edited by Mark Thiessen Nation and Samuel Wells, 211–32. Edinburgh: T. & T. Clark, 2000.

Habel, Norma C. *Reconciliation: Searching for Australia's Soul*. North Blackburn, Vic.: HarperCollins, 1999.

Hacking, Ian, *The Social Construction of What?* Cambridge: Harvard University Press, 1999.

Hall, Douglas John. *Bound and Free: A Theologian's Journey.* Minneapolis: Fortress, 2005.

———. *The Cross in Our Context: Jesus and the Suffering World.* Minneapolis: Fortress, 2003.

———. *God and Human Suffering: An Exercise in the Theology of the Cross.* Minneapolis: Augsburg, 1986.

———. *Professing the Faith: Christian Theology in a North American Context.* Minneapolis: Fortress, 1996.

Hauerwas, Stanley. *Naming the Silences: God, Medicine, and the Problem of Suffering.* Edinburgh: T. & T. Clark, 1993.

———. *Performing the Faith: Bonhoeffer and the Practice of Nonviolence.* Grand Rapids: Brazos, 2004.

———. *With the Grain of the Universe: The Church's Witness and Natural Theology; Being the Gifford Lectures Delivered at the University of St. Andrews in 2001.* Grand Rapids: Brazos, 2001.

Hayes, Victor C., editor. *Toward Theology in an Australian Context.* Bedford Park, SA: Australian Association for the Study of Religions, 1979.

Hillis, Mark, editor and compiler. *Building Partnerships: A Guide to Covenant Renewal with Indigenous People throughout the Uniting Church in Australia.* Sydney: National Assembly of the Uniting Church in Australia, 2008.

Kärkkäinen, Veli-Matti. *An Introduction to Ecclesiology: Ecumenical, Historical & Global Perspectives.* Downers Grove, IL: InterVarsity, 2002.

Jones, Tony. *The New Christians: Dispatches from the Emergent Frontier.* San Francisco: Jossey-Bass, 2008.

Kelly, Tony. *A New Imagining: Towards an Australian Spirituality.* Melbourne: Collins Dove, 1990.

———. "Whither 'Australian Theology'? A Response to Geoffrey Lilburne." *Pacifica* 12 (1999) 192–208.

Kidwell, Clara Sue, et al. *A Native American Theology.* Maryknoll, NY: Orbis, 2001.

Kim, Yung Suk. *Christ's Body in Corinth: The Politics of a Metaphor.* Paul in Critical Contexts. Minneapolis: Fortress, 2008.

Kinast, Robert L. *What Are They Saying about Theological Reflection?* WATSA Series. New York: Paulist, 2000.

Kwok, Pui-Lan. *Introducing Asian Feminist Theology.* Introductions in Feminist Theology 4. Sheffield: Sheffield Academic, 2000.

Lash, Nicholas. *Theology on the Way to Emmaus.* 1986. Reprinted, Eugene, OR: Wipf & Stock, 2005.

Lee, Jung Young. *Marginality: The Key to Multicultural Theology.* Minneapolis: Fortress, 1995.

Lilburn, Geoffrey. "Australian Theology: Protestant Contributions." *Colloquium* 28 (1996) 19–30.

———. "Contextualising Australian Theology: An Enquiry into Method." *Pacifica* 10 (1997) 350–64.

Lindbeck, George A. *The Nature of Doctrine: Religion and Theology in a Postliberal Age.* Louisville: Westminster John Knox, 1984.

Locke, Hubert G. *Searching for God in Godforsaken Times and Places: Reflections on the Holocaust, Racism and Death*. Grand Rapids: Eerdmans, 2003.

McFadyen, Alistair. *Bound to Sin: Abuse, Holocaust and the Christian Doctrine of Sin*. Cambridge Studies in Christian Doctrine 6. Cambridge: Cambridge University Press, 2000.

———. "Truth as Mission: The Christian Claim to Universal Truth in a Pluralistic Public World." *Scottish Journal of Theology*. 46 (1993) 437–56.

McGrath, Alister E., editor. *The Christian Theology Reader*. 2nd ed. Oxford: Blackwell, 2001.

Malone, Peter, co-ordinator. *Discovering an Australian Theology*. Homebush, NSW: St Paul, 1988.

———, editor. *Developing an Australian Theology*. Strathfield, NSW: St Pauls, 1999.

Marsh, Clive. *Christ in Practice: A Christology of Everyday Life*. London: Darton, Longman & Todd, 2006.

Migliore, Daniel L. "Christology in Context." *Interpretation* 49 (1995) 242–54.

———. *Faith Seeking Understanding: An Introduction to Christian Theology*. 2nd ed. Grand Rapids: Eerdmans, 2004.

Minear, Paul S. *Images of the Church in the New Testament*. New Testament Library. Louisville: Westminster John Knox, 2004.

Moltmann, Jürgen. *The Church in the Power of the Spirit: A Contribution to Messianic Ecclesiology*. Translated by Margaret Kohl. London: SCM, 1977.

———. *The Crucified God: The Cross of Christ as the Foundation and Criticism of Christian Theology*. Translated by R. A. Wilson and John Bowden. London: SCM, 1974.

———. *History and the Triune God: Contributions to Trinitarian Theology*. Translated by John Bowden. London: SCM, 1991.

———. *The Spirit of Life: A Universal Affirmation*. Translated by Margaret Kohl. London: SCM, 1992.

Mudge, Lewis S. *The Church as Moral Community: Ecclesiology and Ethics in Ecumenical Debate*. Geneva: World Council of Churches, 1998.

Myers, Ched. *Binding the Strong Man: A Political Reading of Mark's Story of Jesus*. Maryknoll, NY: Orbis, 1995.

———. *Who Will Roll Away the Stone? Discipleship Queries for First World Christians*. Maryknoll, NY: Orbis, 1994.

Nation, Mark Theissen, and Samuel Wells, editors. *Faithfulness and Fortitude: In Conversation with the Theological Ethics of Stanley Hauerwas*. Edinburgh, T. & T. Clark, 2000.

Ng, D. "The Narrative Quality of Experience." *Journal of American Academy of Religion* 39 (1971) 291–311.

Oduyoye, Mercy. "A Biblical Perspective on the Church." *Ecumenical Review* 53 (2001) 44–47.

O'Sullivan, Dominic. *Faith, Politics and Reconciliation: Catholicism and the Politics of Indigeneity*. Adelaide: ATF Press, 2005.

Park, Andrew Sung. *The Wounded Heart of God: The Asian Concept of Han and the Christian Doctrine of Sin*. Nashville: Abingdon, 1993.

Parsons, Susan Frank. "Redeeming Ethics." In *The Cambridge Companion to Feminist Theology*, edited by Susan Frank Parsons 206–23. Cambridge Companions to Religion. Cambridge: Cambridge University Press, 2002.

Pearson, Clive. "Australian Contextual Theologies." In *Asian Christian Theologies: A Research Guide to Authors, Movements, Sources.* Vol. 1, *Asia Regions, 7th–20th Centuries*, edited by John C. England et al., 599–657. Maryknoll, NY: Orbis, 2002.

———, editor. *Faith in a Hyphen: Cross-Cultural Theologies Down Under*. With a Sub-Version by Jione Havea. Adelaide: Openbook, 2004.

Pembroke, Neil. "A Pastoral Perspective on the Suffering God." *Colloquium* 38 (2006) 27–40.

Perkinson, James W. *White Theology: Outing Supremacy in Modernity*. Black Religion, Womanist Thought, Social Justice. New York: Palgrave MacMillan, 2004.

Pinn, Anthony B. *Terror and Triumph: The Nature of Black Religion*. The 2002 Edward Cadbury Lectures. Minneapolis: Fortress, 2003.

Rees, Frank. "Re-cognising the Christ: An Australian Response to John Dominic Crossan." *Colloquium* 31 (1999) 99–109.

Regan, Hilary D. et al., editors. *Christ and Context: The Confrontation between Gospel and Culture*. Edinburgh: T. & T. Clark, 1993.

Report of the Joint Commission between the Roman Catholic Church and the World Methodist Council. *The Apostolic Tradition*. 1986–1991, Fifth Series. Singapore: World Methodist Council, 1991.

———. *Towards a Statement on the Church*. 1982–1986, Fourth Series. Lake Junaluska, NC: World Methodist Council, 1986.

Richard, Lucien. *What Are They Saying about the Theology of Suffering?* WATSA Series. New York: Paulist, 1992.

Rieger, Joerg. *God and the Excluded: Visions and Blind Spots in Contemporary Theology*. Minneapolis: Fortress, 2001.

Ringe, Sharon H. *Jesus, Liberation, and the Biblical Jubilee: Images for Ethics and Christology*. Overtures to Biblical Theology 19. Philadelphia: Fortress, 1985.

Rosenbaum, Alan S., editor. *Is the Holocaust Unique? Perspectives on Comparative Genocide*. Boulder, CO: Westview, 1996.

Russell, Letty M. "Hot-House Ecclesiology: A Feminist Interpretation of the Church." *Ecumenical Review* 53 (2001) 48–56

Sahayadhas, R. "In Search of an Appropriate Ecclesiastical Model." *Bangalore Theological Forum* 34 (2002) 139–58.

Schild, Basil. "God like Whitefella More Better I Reckon." In *Identity, Survival, Witness: Reconfiguring Theological Agendas*, edited by Karen L. Bloomquist, 51–57. Theology in the Life of the Church 3. Geneva: Lutheran World Federation, 2008.

Schreiter, Robert J. *Constructing Local Theologies*. London: SCM, 1985.

Searle, John, *The Construction of Social Reality*. New York: Free Press, 1995.

Segundo, Juan Luis. *Jesus of Nazareth Yesterday and Today*. Vol. 1, *Faith and Ideologies*. Translated by John Drury. Melbourne: Dove, 1984.

Smith, Andrea. "Dismantling the Master's Tools with the Master's House: Native Feminist Liberation Theologies." *Journal of Feminist Religious Studies* 22 (2006) 85–97.

Soelle, Dorothee. "Suffering from a Feminist Perspective." In *What Are They Saying about the Theology of Suffering,* edited by Lucien Richard, 73–88. WATSA Series. New York, Paulist, 1992.

Storrar, William F., and Andrew R. Morton, editors. *Public Theology for the 21st Century: Essays in Honour of Duncan B. Forrester.* London: T. & T. Clark, 2004.

Tamez, Elsa. "An Ecclesial Community: Women's Visions and Voices." *Ecumenical Review* 5 (2001) 57–63.

Tanner, Kathryn. *Theories of Culture: A New Agenda for Theology.* Guides to Theological Inquiry. Minneapolis: Fortress, 1997.

Tanner, Mary. "On Being Church: Some Thoughts Inspired by the Ecumenical Community." *The Ecumenical Review* 53 (2001) 64–71.

Thistlethwaite, Susan Brooks. "Christology and Postmodernism: Not Everyone Who Says to Me, 'Lord, Lord.'" *Interpretation* 49 (1995) 267–80.

Thomas, Linda E., editor. *Living Stones in the Household of God: The Legacy and Future of Black Theology.* Minneapolis: Fortress, 2004.

Uniting Church in Australia. *The Basis of Union.* 1992 ed. Collingwood, Vic.: Uniting Church Press, 1992.

Volf, Miroslav. *After Our Likeness: The Church as the Image of the Trinity.* Sacra Doctrina. Grand Rapids: Eerdmans, 1998.

———. *Exclusion and Embrace: A Theological Exploration of Identity, Otherness, and Reconciliation.* Nashville: Abingdon, 1996.

———. "The Social Meaning of Reconciliation." *Interpretation* 54 (2000) 158–72.

Volf, Miroslav, and Dorothy C. Bass, editors. *Practicing Theology: Beliefs and Practices in Christian Life.* Grand Rapids: Eerdmans, 2002.

Watson, Natalie K. *Introducing Feminist Ecclesiology.* Introductions in Feminist Theology 10. Cleveland: Pilgrim, 2002.

Welker, Michael "Who is Jesus Christ for Us Today?" *Harvard Theological Review* 95 (2002) 129–46.

Wells, Samuel. *Improvisation: The Drama of Christian Ethics.* Grand Rapids: Brazos, 2004.

Williams, Rowan, "The Spiritual and the Religious: Is the Territory Changing?" Lecture delivered at Westminster Cathedral in Faith and Life in Britain series, April 17, 2008. Online: http://www.archbishopofcanterbury.org/1759/.

Wraight, Geoff. "Contours of an Australian Christology: A Christological Conversation with Issues of Belonging and Identity in Australian Consciousness." MTh minor thesis. Melbourne College of Divinity, 2000.

Wright, N. T. *Evil and the Justice of God.* Downers Grove, IL: InterVarsity, 2006.

Yoder, John Howard. *Preface to Theology: Christology and Theological Method.* Grand Rapids: Brazos, 2002.

———. *The Royal Priesthood: Essays Ecclesiological and Ecumenical.* Edited and Introduced by Michael G. Cartwright. Grand Rapids: Eerdmans, 1994.